THE HELIAND

UNIVERSITY OF NORTH CAROLINA
STUDIES IN THE GERMANIC LANGUAGES
AND LITERATURES

Publication Committee

FREDERIC E. COENEN, EDITOR

WERNER P. FRIEDERICH   GEORGE S. LANE

JOHN G. KUNSTMANN   HERBERT W. REICHERT

For other volumes in this series see page 206.

Foreign Sales through:
Librairie E. Droz
8 Rue Verdaine
Geneva, Switzerland

NUMBER FIFTY-TWO

UNIVERSITY
OF NORTH CAROLINA
STUDIES IN
THE GERMANIC LANGUAGES
AND LITERATURES

THE HELIAND

translated from the Old Saxon

by

MARIANA SCOTT

CHAPEL HILL

THE UNIVERSITY OF NORTH CAROLINA PRESS

Printed in the Netherlands by Royal VanGorcum Ltd., Assen

FOREWORD

Every translation is perforce an interpretation, influenced not only by the personality as well as the training of the translator, but by the age of which he is a product. The best a conscientious translator can do, unless his translation is to become a mere soulless, colorless prose retelling of the original, is to try to become attuned to the mind and the times of the author with whom he is working and then to attempt to reproduce a semblance at least of the melody he hears. He is aware that he must make certain compromises: neither a literal translation nor one which concentrates on the externals of the metrics will reproduce the ideas and emotions which he knows are present. He is constantly forced to adapt and to shape. Yet with the adapting and shaping, too, there is inevitably a loss.

It is with these things in mind that I began my work on that anonymous 9th century Old Saxon masterpiece, the *Heliand*. After discarding an attempt to confine my vocabulary as much as possible to Anglo-Saxon roots, I settled on a somewhat archaic style as most appropriate for reproducing not only the biblical but somewhat primitive, naive atmosphere of the original. Christ, for example, is frequently called the "Bairn of God." Words like "weeds" for "clothing," "quick" for "alive" have been used — often, however, with the more usual word in the repetition. The various pronominal forms of "thee," "thou," and "ye" have been regularly employed. Since they are so essential to the Old Saxon style, the kennings have been retained wherever possible. So have the repetitions. The name, "Heliand," one of the kennings for Christ and therefore source of the title, has caused some difficulty. "Savior" has become for us a rather colorless word, having few of the connotations of the Old Saxon "Heliand." I have therefore used the translation, "Healer," since so often the emphasis is on His healing both of men's bodies and also their souls.

vii

It was important for me to remember that the *Heliand* was originally intended for recitation. This accounts for the very great emphasis on rhythm. While the exact form of the old alliterative verse, though common to both early English and German poetry, proved too confining, a freer adaptation was possible. Let us remember that much of the effect of modern free verse depends on the interplay of sounds: assonance and alliteration. Keeping in mind the purpose of the original, I read my translation aloud as I worked, repeating lines several times, varying and checking rhythms, trying to imitate the surge of the meter and yet avoid monotony. The end result was a line of variable feet, usually a rather free alternation of anapests and iambics with a few scattered tribrachs and spondees, divided by the traditional caesura. I aimed for an alliteration of at least one accented syllable in the first half line with one accented syllable in the second half. If more sounded right, I was delighted. If none worked, I tried to make the rhythm carry the line along to the next cadence. Not all of it, I painedly admit, turned out to be poetry — but then not all of the Old Saxon is!

In the course of my work, I also tried to make a study of the sounds which were dominant in the Old Saxon. By far the most common was the alliteration of "w," followed by "l," "m" and, for certain effects, "s," "b" and the plosives. Since the heavy "w" sound carried the weight of the meter, it was important for me to reproduce it as often as possible. I had good precedent: the Old Saxon author often padded his lines for the same reason with some form of *willeon* or with such formulas as *mit wordun*, or *wordo eftha werco*. Using my precedent, I therefore translated such words as *werod* or *wer* as "world folk" and *world man*, sometimes even — if sense permitted — as "war-folk" or "warrior," etc. *Waldand*, as an epithet of God or Christ, became "the Wielder." Search for alliteration sometimes even led the Old Saxon poet astray. A very good example of that would be *that graf an theson griote* — "grave on the sand," after the grave had been described as hewn in the rock. In such a case I considered a translation, "grave in the grotto," not too far from the point. There are many other such cases, though in general I tried to keep as close to the original as possible, both in meaning and in style.

Lastly, I wish to thank all those who have read, criticized, and corrected my translation in the six years of my labor. Most especially however, my gratitude is directed to Dr. Philip M. Palmer, now of the University of California at Berkeley, who not only introduced me to the fascination of the *Heliand* many, many years ago, but undertook the onerous task of checking the many passages about which I still had some doubt.

MARIANA SCOTT

HELIAND

I

Many there were   tensing their minds
To say what was whispered: that Might-Wielding Christ
Had here among men   done miracles many
With His words and His works.   Wise men aplenty,
People of earth — all would praise   the preachings of
Christ,
God's holy Word,   and write with their hands
Bright in a book   how best God's bidding
They might carry out,   the kith of mankind.
There were four from the many: they had might from the
Maker,
Help, too, from Heaven   and from the Holy Ghost,
Strength from the Savior: so were they chosen for this.
Singly they were to inscribe   the Gospel there in a book,
Committing to writing   so many commandments of God,
Holy, heavenly Word: nor dared any here,
Any child of man,   emulate them, these four,
Picked for the task   by the power of God:
Matthew and Mark,   as these men were called,
Luke, also John —   they were beloved of God.
Worthy were they for the work.   The Wide-Wielder
Had filled the hearts of the heroes   with the Holy
Ghost,
Perfectly all   with pious opinion,
And wise words many   and still more of wit,
That they should begin   the goodly Gospel
With their holy voices,   raise it on high —

The Word in this world   which has nowhere a like:
That it praise Him ever,   the Prince All-powerful,
The Lord who layeth low   the loathsome thing,
Who doth stamp out all sin   and the hate of Satan,
Withstandeth the strife.   For He is strong of mind,
Mild, too, and good —   He who is Master of these,
Aethling and Maker,   Almighty Lord.
So were those four   to inscribe with their fingers,
Set down and sing   and say forth boldly
That of Christ's might and His strength   much had they
                heard
And had seen indeed,   which He Himself had here spoken;
Proclaimed and accomplished   miracles countless,
As He Himself had promised —   He, Wielder of Power,
Wide Ruling Lord —   when He first shaped world,
Surrounding it all   with a single Word,
Heaven and earth   and all that they held,
Full-worked or still waxing: with God's Word
All was encompassed   and set forth accordingly
Which world-men should rule   over widest lands
And when each age of this earth   should come to its end.
There was still one before them —   for five had slipped
                by
For the kinsmen of earth —   and now the sixth was to
                come,
Blessed by God's strength   and the birth of Christ,
Best of All Healers,   and the Holy Ghost,
Come to this mid-world   to help the many,
The world-children all   'gainst the wiles of the Fiend
And his secret snares.   So to the Roman folk
Had Lord God granted   the greatest of realms,
Had strengthened the heart   of the crowds of the host,
So that they laid low   much land-folk all over.
Their helm-wearers had rule   from the city of Rome,
Their leaders had power   in every land o'er the people
                there,
Over the heathens all.   Herod was chosen

King of Jerusalem   over the Jew-folk.
Caesar in Rome's city,   the mighty ruler,
Had set him there 'mid his thanes.   Verily, though,
He was not kin to the clanships   of Israel, not come
From their best-born;   but his bounty he had
Through the grace of Caesar   straight from the Rome-
                                        burg,
So that then the fighting men,   famed for their fierce-
                                        ness,
The children of Israel,   friends changeless in strength,
Were subject to him,   since he held sway —
Herod — over kinships   and councillors
Of Israel's landsmen.   There lived there then
An aged man, a wise man   of reasonable mind:
He was come from the people   of the clan of Levi,
The famed son of Jacob   of a very fair family:
Zachery he was hight,   was so holy a man,
For he gladly did give   service unto God,
Worked to His will.   So did his wife —
She was already a very old crone,   and no offspring
Had been granted to them   in their youth.
They lived without fault,   warding God's love,
Were humbly submissive   to the King of Heaven,
Praising our Prince;   nor practiced they evil
Among mankind;   nor did any meanness,
Neither fault nor sin.   Still were they sorrowed of
                                        soul,
Since not ever could they   be granted an heir:
Bereft they of bairns.   The bidding of God
He did in Jerusalem.   As oft as his duty
And the rightness of time   did remind him thereof,
So oft did he hie himself hence   to the holy place,
To the High One's temple,   to the Heaven-King's house,
To serve Him all selfless   and make sacrifice,
Yearning to work   with a God-wise mind.

The time was then come —   as they did tell it,
Wise men with words —   that Zachery should stand
watch
There in God's temple.   Many were gathered
In Jerusalem there   of the folk of the Jews,
Hordes in the holy place.   Most humbly they begged
Might-Wielding God   for His grace,
The Lord of All Heaven   to release them from evil.
The folk stood around by the holy house,   and the
high-born man
Entered the temple.   The others all,
The folk stayed outside   of the sanctuary,
The host of the Hebrew,   till the holy man
Had worked and had done   the All-Wielder's will.
As he took the incense,   the sage in the temple,
Round the altar the censer,   to serve his Liege —
Piously labored   for his own dear Lord;
And gladly he served   in God's thralldom
With a generous heart,   as one should joyously
Follow one's master.   There a fright befell him,
Terror there in the temple.   Trembling he espied
God's angel inside   there in the sanctuary.
And he spoke to the sage,   said with words not to fear
Nor to have any dread.   "For thy deeds," quoth he,
"Are of worth to the Wielder   and thy words as well.
Thy thralldom has earned thee His thanks,   since thou hast
believed in Him
And in His strength alone.   I am His angel,
And Gabriel I am hight.   Ever I stand before God,
Stand in the Almighty's sight,   except that He send
me forth
On some errand for Him.   And now He hight me fare forth,
Bade me to tell thee,   that to thee a babe will be born
From thy aged wife.   In this world shall be given unto
thee:

4

Wise he of word.   Of wine he shall never partake,
In life neither of wine nor of cider.   So have the Weird
                    Ones set down:
The Measurers have marked it   and the might of God.
He bade that I tell thee: he shall be thane
To the Heaven-King's Self;   bade that ye hold him
And faithfully foster him.   Quoth that he would find
Honors so many   up in God's kingdom.
Quoth that the good man   should be called John.
Commanded that ye   so call it, that child,
When it doth come.   Quoth that Christ's thane
It was to become   in this wide, wide world,
Thane of His Own Son.   And quoth that they both
Betake themselves here   swiftly for tidings."
Zachery then spoke   and said to God's angel,
Beginning to wonder   about his deeds and his words:
"How can that so   come to pass?" quoth he,
"So late in our lives?   For us 'tis too late
To win such rewards   as thy words have spoken.
For we two were equal of age: twenty winters
Here in this world,   when this woman did come unto me;
And together we have shared   for seventy winters
Both board and bed,   since I chose her my bride.
In our youth we acquired   no offspring, no heir,
Could beget no babe   in our bedchamber —
Now that we are old,   and age has robbed us of deed-
                    strength —
Dulled is our sight   and slow are our loins,
Our flesh falleth away,   our skin is unfair,
Our limbs unlithe,   withered our once-live bodies,
And our appearance: alas, 'tis altered —
Mind both and might: so many a day
We have wandered this world.   Methinks 'twere a wonder
If it ever so happed,   as thou hast said with thy words."

Then the Heaven-King's herald　　was hurt in his mind
That Zachery should wonder　　so at His works
And would not believe　　that Holy Lord God,
If He so willed it,　　could well make him young,
As once he had been.　　So the angel chastised him,
The sage, so that he could not say　　e'en a single word,
Nor speak with his mouth　　"until thy son is come,
Sprung from thy old wife,　　an earl and shining,
Until a young bairn is born　　to the best of clans
Here in this world.　　Then shalt thou again speak words.
Thy voice shall have strength.　　Nor shalt thou be
　　　　　　　　　　　silent
For any time longer."　　And straightway it was
What the Almighty's angel　　had there uttered,
Had told in the temple:　　that became true.
Bereft of speech　　was the sage,
Though a clear mind　　he bore in his breast.
All day they bided　　before the God-house, the folk —
And they wondered all,　　why this praiseworthy man,
This sage should need so long　　to serve his Master,
As never did other thanes　　in the Lord's thralldom
Make such sacrifice with their hands　　there in the
　　　　　　　　　　　sanctuary.
Lo: the ancient sage　　did leave the temple.
The earls thronged nearer.　　There was longing in them,
To hear what he would say　　most soothly to them,
How wise he would guide them.　　But no word could he
　　　　　　　　　　　speak
Nor say to his retainers;　　but with his right hand
He instructed the folk　　to follow God's teachings.
The folk understood　　that verily he had seen
Some token from God,　　though he could not tell them
Nor show them the truth.　　There in his turn
He had worked full well　　our Wide-Wielder's service,
As 'twas marked among men.　　Soon God's might was made
　　　　　　　　　　　known,

God's strength and His skill: for the crone so aged,
The wife was with child.   Offspring was granted unto
                              them,
Bairn in the bastion —   a so God-like babe.
And the woman awaited   the workings of Weird.
The winter wore on,   the year fell away. John came,
A light to the earth-folk: fair was his flesh,
Seemly his skin,   and shimmering was he of cheek,
And the hair of his head   and his nails. Now the
                              hoary,
The wise gathered quickly,   the closest of kinsmen,
Wondering much at the work,   how well it could happen
That a couple so aged   could still bear a child,
A babe in the bastion,   unless at God's bidding.
They well understood   that unless this was so,
It could never have been —   this babe — quite so fair.
Then an old man spoke,   one of learned and reasonable
                              mind,
Who knew wise words.   With zeal he did ask
What the babe's name should be   here below in this
                              world:
"Methinks in his way and his bearing   he is greater
                              than we.
So I wean that verily God from Heaven   hath sent him
                              Himself."
Then the child's mother did straightway speak. She who
                              had borne him did say
With the babe on her lap: "Last year God's bidding
Did come unto us,   commanded with words of great weight
That he be called John,   according to the teaching of
                              God.
Even, indeed, if I might,   in my mind I cannot,
I dare not so change it."   Then spoke thereupon
A most haughty man: from her homeland he was,
"No aethling is named so," quoth he,   "no kith of our
                              clan.

Now then! Let us choose us   another, a nicer name.
Later indeed he will like it,   if he is so able."
Again spoke the elder,   who there could say much:
"I can never counsel   any knight whatever
To alter God's word.   Let us ask the old man,
The father, who sitteth wisely   in his wine-hall there.
Though he cannot speak,   say a single word,
He may with his book-letters   make us some writing,
May spell us a name."   Now he came nearer,
Laid a book on his lap   and bade him to write,
To set down wisely   with word-mark and sign
What they were to name him,   that holy babe.
He took the book in his hand,   thought in his heart
Right gladly of God   and writ the name John —
Wisely he worked it: and with words thereupon
He did speak unto them,   and shrewdly indeed.
Once more he had power to speak,   had wisdom and way.
His pain was now past,   his punishment dire.
God the Mighty had so made it   that in his mind
He could not so soon forget Him,   should He again send
                    His herald.

I V

'Twas not long thereafter   that all came to pass,
As Almighty God   had promised mankind:
That He would send   the Son of Himself,
The Heavenly Bairn,   here to this world,
So that He might save   the folk all from sin,
The clansmen from hell-pangs.   There came His herald,
Gabriel, down   to Galilee-land,
The All-Wielder's angel,   where he knew a woman of
                    worth,
A maiden right mild.   She was called Mary.
The girl was grown.   To a man of good clan,
To a thane hight Joseph   her troth she had given,
The daughter of David.   A dear wife was she,

A graceful woman and good.   There the angel of God
In Nazareth-burg   did greet her by name;
Stood there before her   and spoke to her for Lord God:
"Hail to thee, Mary!" quoth he,   "Loved by the Maker
                         art thou!
Aye, worthy art thou of the Wielder,   for thou hast
                         wisdom,
Lady, gifted with grace.   Glorified art thou ever
Above all women.   Be thou not weakly of mind,
Nor fearful of heart.   I come not to hurt
Nor to bring thee a gull-thing.   Thou shalt be our
                         God's,
Be our Master's mother   here among men, bearing a man-
                         child,
Son of the Heaven-King.   His name shall be Healer
Here mid the earth-folk.   His end cometh not,
Nor hath whereover He ruleth   ever an end — His realm —
He, Finest of Folk-Leaders."   The fairest of women,
The maiden then answered   unto God's angel,
The loveliest among ladies.   "Lo, how may that be?"
                         quoth she,
"That I shall bring forth a son?   Never knew I man in
                         my life."
The All-Wielder's angel   had ready his word
To answer the maid.   "From the meadows of sky
The Holy Ghost shall descend   through the strength of
                         God.
From Him will a Wee One   be granted thee here in this
                         world.
The Wielder's strength   will o'ershadow thee,
The Heaven-King   All High with His shade.
Below was never   a birth so fair,
Never so wonderous down among men.   For from God's
                         might
It cometh here to this world."   The heart of the woman
                         was again
Utterly turned to God's will   at these tidings.

"All ready stand I,"   quoth she, "for such service,
If He will so have me.   His handmaid am I.
I trust in these things.   Therefore let it then hap,
As thou sayest with thy word,   as is His will,
My Lord's, my God's.   My mind doubteth not,
Nor my word nor my way."   So I heard that the woman
Received God's tidings   all gladly indeed
With a shimmering soul,   with bright shining truth
And faith clear and fair.   The Holy Ghost became
The Babe in her womb;   and in her breast,
In her heart itself she understood.   She said to all
                                  whom she wished,
That she had conceived   through the All-Wielder's
                                  strength,
Holy from Heaven.   Then was Joseph's heart,
His mind right worried.   For this maiden,
This pious woman,   this high-born wife
He had bought as his bride.   He knew she had bairn with-
                                  in her,
Yet he thought not a whit   but that his wife
Had kept herself carefully.   He could not yet know
The Wielder's blithe tidings.   But to make her his
                                  bride
He no longer wished,   his wife in his halls.
And thus he began   to think in his mind
How he might forsake her,   yet cause her no hardship nor
                                  sorrow.
He wanted it not noised   nor known about
Among the many. He feared   that the children of men
Would bereave her of life.   For this was the land-way,
The hallowed, old law   of the Hebrew folk:
Whensoever a woman   was unrightly wed,
She must pay with her life   for this bedship.
Never was lady so good   that she could long live
Mid the land-folk,   could live 'mid the world-lords.
Then in his mind the wise man,   the good man, Joseph,
Began to bethink himself   of these things,

How he might slyly   forsake the girl.
'Twas not long thereafter   that the Almighty's angel
Hurried to him in a dream,   the Heaven-King's herald,
And bade him keep her   and care for her well
And love her, too, in his mind.   "At Mary," quoth he,
                    "thy maid,
Be not thou wrathful;   she is a right good wife.
Scorn her not sternly.   Thou shalt hold her
And ward her well   in the world, as before,
Fostering thy love-pledge   and thy friendship as well.
Nor let her be loathsome to thee,   though she hath
                    Bairn 'neath her limbs,
A babe in her womb.   Through God's bidding It cometh,
Through the Holy Ghost   from the Heaven-heath here.
Jesus Christ is that Babe!   God's own Bairn shall He be,
The All-Wielder's Son.   Thou shalt hold Him well
With holiness, too.   Nor let thy heart doubt,
Nor thy mind be disturbed."   Then the man's heart
Was turned by these words,   so that he again won love
                    for this woman,
For the maid, Marie.   God's might he now understood,
The Wielder's bidding.   Great was his will,
That he should hold her,   in holiness keep her.
He cared for her in his home.   And she carried all
                    cleanly
The Holy Ghost —   all for God's glory,
The Man of Goodness,   until God's fate-word
Reminded her mightily   that unto the light of mankind
She should bring Him,   the Best of all Bairns.

v

There came from Rome-burg   from the mighty man
Over the earth-folk,   from Octavian himself,
Ban and bidding   over his broad fealty;
This was come from Caesar   unto every king:
To the home-sitting ones   as far as the war-lords

Wielded their power   o'er the people and land.
'Twas hight that all men   habited outside their own
                    boroughs
Should seek now their homeland,   all heroes their heritage,
To bide their lord's heralds;   each landsman should go
Quickly to the clan   of his kinsmen,
To the burg of his birth.   The ban was proclaimed
Over this wide, wide world.   And the world-folk did
                    gather,
In every bastion the men all.   The messengers fared
                    forth,
Those come from Caesar,   book-learned thanes.
And neatly they wrote   each name on a scroll,
Both land and the man,   so that no lord could avoid it,
No man his tax;   but all must pay tribute,
The heroes each for his head.   So to his homeland
Came Joseph, the good man,   as God the Almighty,
The Wielder had willed it;   with his family he came,
Sought his shining castle,   his lordly seat,
The bastion at Bethlehem,   where they both did dwell,
Hero and holy maid,   Mary the good.
There stood in earlier days   the shining throne
Of the high-born king,   of the earl of the Hebrews,
Of David the good,   as long as he governed
And kept lofty seat.   They were his kith,
Were come from his clan,   were of good kin all,
Both through their birth.   Then I heard that the bright
                    tidings
Admonished Mary,   and the might of God:
That on this site   a Son should be hers,
Born here in Bethlehem,   the Mightiest of Bairns,
The Strongest of Kings.   Come was the Shining One,
Mighty here to man's light,   as for many a day
Pictures of Him   and tokens aplenty
Had foretold in this world.   So all had turned true,
As the sages had spoken it   in the long, long ago.
Through His Own Self's strength,   how most surely He would
                    come

To this earth-realm here —   with humility — He,
Protector to many.   Then His mother did take Him,
And she swaddled Him well,   the fairest of women,
With garments and goodly gems.   With her two gracious
                                  hands
She lovingly laid Him,   the Little Man,
The Child in the crib,   though He had God's strength,
The Master of Men.   There His mother sat by Him,
The woman there waking;   she herself warded Him,
Held there the Holy Bairn;   and her heart doubted not —
The mind of the maid.   It became known to the many
Over this wide, wide world.   The warders did hear it:
Grooms were they there,   keeping guard outside,
Were war-men on watch;   with the horses they were,
With the beasts in the field.   And lo: before them they
                                  saw
The darkness divide in the air.   Down came God's light —
Through the clouds came shining,   surrounding the grooms
Afar in the fields.   And sorely they feared,
These men, in their minds.   Then God's mighty angel
They saw coming afar.   To them together he spoke,
Hight that the grooms   not dread any grief
From the light. "For lo!"   quoth he, "A glad thing
I tell you and truly,   long longed-for tidings
Bespeaking great power: for in this selfsame night
Christ, Blessed Bairn of our own God,   is born in the
                                  bastion of David,
He — our Master All Good.   That is joy to mankind,
The weal of all folk.   So that ye may find
The Mightiest of Babes   in Bethlehem-burg,
Take this as a token   that I now tell unto you
With soothy words: that He lieth swaddled,
A Child in a crib,   though He be King
Over earth and heaven   and the children of men,
All-Wielder o'er World."   Verily as he spoke this word,
There was come with   this single one of the angels
A multitude down   from the meadows of Heaven —

A holy host,   the fair folk of God.
They spoke, lauded greatly   the Lord of Mankind.
They raised holy song,   as they returned through the
                    clouds
To the meadows of Heaven.   And the warders did hear
How the great host of angels   gave praise unto Almighty
                    God
With these words most reverently: "Honor be" quoth
                    they,
"To our Lord Himself in the highest,   to the King of
                    Heaven —
And on earth be peace   to all children of men,
To folk of good will   who accept their God
With hearts ever pure."   The herdsmen understood
That a mighty thing   had admonished them:
Blithe tidings there.   They turned back to Bethlehem
That selfsame night,   for their spirits longed
Most greatly to see   Christ Himself.

VI

The angel of God had shown   unto them the shining token,
So that they themselves —   they could wander forth
To the Bairn of God.   Straightway they found Him, the
                    Babe,
The Lord of Mankind,   the Master of Peoples.
They praised God the Wielder,   and with their words
They made known far and wide   in the shining castle
What tokens holy they had seen indeed   from the meadows
                    of Heaven,
What signs there, fair in the field.   The woman full well
Kept these things in her heart,   the holy virgin,
The maid in her mind: whatever she heard the men there
                    saying.
Fittingly she reared Him,   the fairest of women;
With her love the mother   did raise the Master of Men,
The Holy Heavenly Bairn.   The heroes did speak

On the eighth day,   the earls of the kingdom,
Very wise men all,   with the handmaid of God:
That His name should be "Healer,"   as the Heaven King's
                              herald,
As God's holy angel,   Gabriel had spoken,
Had bade the woman   with words of truth,
When she first conceived Him,   so fair in this world.
God's angel she followed,   and right gladly, too.
For great was her will   to hold Him in holiness.
The year strode on,   till the Peace-Child of God
Had forty days and as many nights, too.   There a deed
                              needed doing;
To Jerusalem they must take Him,   to the Wielder's
                              temple.
That was the way then,   the world-folk's custom,
Which no Hebrew woman   would dare to neglect,
But that when she had brought forth   her first-born son
She needs must take him   to the Lord God's temple.
So they did travel, Mary   and Joseph, the good folk twain,
Both from Bethlehem.   The Babe they had with them,
The Holy Christ.   They sought then God's house
In Jerusalem; they accomplished   the custom of Jew-folk,
Made sacrifice unto the Wielder   there in His sanctuary,
To God in His temple.   There they found them a good man,
An old one, hard by the altar —   aethling-born he —
So many summers and winters   had he spent in the temple,
Lived in the light,   working God's love
With a clean soul.   Holy spirit he had
And a joyous heart.   Simon was he hight;
Long had the Lord's power   pointed out to him
That he would not leave   the light of this world,
Until 'twould be granted him   to see with his eyes
Holy Christ Himself,   the King of the Heaven.
His heart was most blithe in his breast,   when he saw the
                              Bairn
Coming into the temple.   He gave thanks to the Wielder,
To Almighty God,   that with his eyen he had seen It.

To Him he did go and gladly received Him,
The old man with his arms: all well he did know
The sign and the symbol,   and the Child of God,
The Heaven-King Holy.   "Now, Lord," quoth he,
"I gladly shall bid Thee,   since aged I be,
To let me, Thy most humble thane,   take leave from
                here,
To fare forth in Thy peace   to where my forebears
                did dwell,
Folk in this world,   since my wish is fulfilled —
The dearest of days: I did see my Liege,
The Loveliest of Lords,   as long, long ago
It was promised unto me.   To all peoples
Thou art the Light —   great Light to all heathen
                lands,
Who have not yet accepted   the All-Wielder's power.
Thy coming, o Master of mine,   O my Lord, my dear Lord,
Is glory and honor   to Israel's children,
To Thine own landfolk,   Thy beloved people."
Secretly then the old man   there at the altar
Spoke to the good woman,   truly did tell her
How her Son would become   to some certain ruin,
To some consolation,   to the children of men —
A love-thing to those   who list to His teaching,
But harm yet to them,   refusing to hearken
To the gospel of Christ.   "Thou shalt suffer," quoth
                he, "great care
And hurt in thy heart,   when the earth-children
                here
Will kill Him with weapons.   This thy great work will
                be:
To suffer this sorrow."   The Maid understood all,
The wise man's words.   There came, too, a woman
From inside the temple.   Anna was she called,
Was Phanuck's daughter.   Full well her Lord had she
                served
With a grateful heart,   was an excellent woman.

16

After her maidenhood,   when a man's wife she became,
An earl's on his estate,   this excellent girl,
With her husband   she had held sway
Seven years o'er his lands.   I heard that she then suffered
                                         grief:
That the great might   of the Measurer
Did divide them, Weird   most woeful. A widow,
She dwelt in the temple   eighty and four
Winters here in the world.   Well she had served Him,
                                         her God
And her Lord, day and night,   never leaving the temple.
She, too, came to this selfsame place.   Straightway she
                                         saw —
She knew God's Holy Bairn,   to the heroes announced it,
To the folk at the altar,   this spell all welcome.
Said that so near   was the Savior's salvation,
The help of the Heaven King.   "Now Holy Christ,
The All-Wielder Himself,   is come to the sanctuary
To deliver the folk   who have bided so long,
So many a while   in this mid-world here —
Poor people they —   so that in this present thing
Mankind all may rejoice."   Many were joyous,
The world-folk there in the temple: they heard the glad
                                         tidings
Spoken by God.   The woman had ended the sacrifice,
As her vow and the book   in the shining bastion had
                                         told her,
Her handwork most holy.   They went on home
To Jerusalem,   Mary and Joseph,
The Holy Family.   They had the Heaven-King
At their landhouse ever,   the Son of the Lord,
Protector of many.   Thus to the people it was not made
                                         known —
Not further known in the world;   but so was His will,
The Heaven-King's mind.

VII

Although all holy men
Recognized Christ,   at the court of the king
It was not yet known to the men   who in their minds
Were not rightly inclined;   rather concealed from them
With words and with works,   until the wise ones,
Those men from the East   did come to the folk,
Swift lords on the long way   over the land.
Bright beacon they followed   and sought God's Bairn;
And with pureness of soul   they purposed to kneel
And confess themselves   as His thanes.
So they brought to pass   the Providence of God.
When they found Herod   enthroned on high,
King, speaking slime-words,   as mighty he sat
Mad with his men,   ever anxious for murder —
They addressed him gravely   in kingly wise,
In his house the sages;   and straightway he asked them
What business   had brought them out here,
These war-men from far, far away.   "Whether ye carry
                    wound gold
To give to some man?   To whom are ye going,
Travelling on foot? What?   I know not whence ye come
                    from afar,
Earls of another folk.   I see ye art aethling born,
Kin of good clan.   Never before are come here
Such envoys from another land,   since over this folk of
                    men
I have wielded my power   in this great, wide realm.
Ye shall tell me truly   before these retainers
Why ye art come   indeed to this land."
They answered in turn,   the men from the East,
Word-wise warriors.   "We can," quoth they,
"Most easily tell thee   our business with truth,
Rightly reveal why we are come   here on this road
From the east of this earth.   Aethlings were there,
Good speaking men,   who promised us good

And help aplenty   from the King of Heaven
Verily with their words.   There was a wise man there,
Hoary and sage —   so long ago was that now —
Our ancestor there in the East —   nor has any man since
                                    then
Ever spoken so sharply.   God's spell he could tell,
For the Lord of the Land-people   had lent him the gift
To hearken up   from the earth
To the All-Wielder's word.   His wisdom was great,
The thoughts of that thane.   Then when he was to depart,
To forfeit his home   and the crowd of the human folk,
Forsaking the life of the landsmen —   and seek the
                                other light:
Then he called his followers   all to come closer —
His heirs were they there —   and to the earls
He most soothly said   what is since then come,
Hath happed in this world: A Wise King would come here,
Mighty and shining   come to the mid-world,
Best by His birth;   quoth that God's Bairn He would be;
Quoth that in this world   He would wield power
Eternally through all of time   over heaven and earth;
Said that on the self-same day,   when He — so blessed —
Was born to His mother   on this mid-world here —
So quoth he — in the East   would shine a single white
                                    star,
In the heavens on high,   such as never before we have
                                    had
Between earth and heaven   or anywhere else:
Neither such Bairn   nor such beacon bright;
That three men from the people   should go offer prayer;
Hight them think well   when they would see God's beacon
Rise in the East, hight   they should ready themselves
                                straightway;
Hight that we should follow   where'er it might fare
Westward over the world.   Now well it hath happed,
Come through God's power: a King is born,
Bold He and strong.   We have seen the beacon shining
                                    bright

Over Heaven's stars.   So I know Holy God,
The Mighty One, hath marked it Himself.   Every morn we
     did see it,
This brilliant star shining.   So we followed the bea-
     con here,
The while through ways and through woods.   That was
     our greatest wish —
To see Him ourselves,   to know where to seek Him,
The King in this kingdom.   Tell us to which clan He is
     born."

There arose in Herod's breast   a great rage 'round his
     heart.
Spirit and heart began to seethe   with sorrow within him,
For he heard them say that he   should now have a Head
     over him,
A mightier King   and One of good clan,
Blessed 'mongst His folk.   Then he ordered them all
To gather together,   what good men there were,
In Jerusalem the wisest   with their speech and their
     words,
And in their breasts   in book-craft
Most verily learned.   And he asked them with words,
Most anxiously asked them — this evil-souled man,
The king of the people —   where Christ would be born
In this world-realm here,   the Peace-Wielder Good.
Then the folk replied,   the people most truly;
Quoth that they knew   quite well that He
Would be born in Bethlehem.   "So 'tis writ in our books
And wisely inscribed,   as the truth-sayers,
Those full wise sages,   have spoken it further:
That from Bethlehem   the Herdsman of Bastions,
The Loved Warder of Land   should come to the light;
The Counselor of Clans   should come to His rule
O'er the hordes of the land-folk;   and His grace will
     hover
Mild o'er this mid-world   for the peoples many."

VIII

There I heard that as soon   as the evil-souled king
Told the truth-sayers' word   to the travellers, the earls
                    from abroad
Those faring from far —   he questioned them fully,
When first on the east-path   they had then seen it —
The king-star acoming,   the token all clear,
Bright and high in the sky.   They wished to hide nothing
                    from him
And truly they told him.   He hight them travel,
Go forth on their way;   hight that they fathom the news
Of the New Child's coming;   and the king himself,
The master of Jews,   gave order most sternly
To the wise men three   that when they fared from the
                    West,
That they should give him account   where he could seek
                    that King
In His hall and His home.   Quoth that he with his thanes
Wished to reverence the Bairn.   But he thought to become
His slayer by the weapon's edge.   Yet All-Wielding God
Was minded elsewise.   He could accomplish,
Could finish far more in this light: for that shines
                    still long —
The prophesied power of God!   There appeared the symbol
Clear 'neath the clouds.   Those men, wise and clever,
                    made ready
To travel. They fared   forth now from there,
Bold on their mission.   They would seek God's Bairn,
They themselves and alone.   No thralls had they with
                    them,
But they were just three: well versed in such things,
Were indeed clever men,   who came carrying their gifts.
Then they saw it so wisely   shining forth 'neath the
                    clouds,
High in the heavens,   where fared the white stars.
They recognized clearly the beacon of God —   through
                    Christ it was worked

Here in the world.   The world-men went following it,
Full piously thence.   Those who could further them,
Until they well saw,   these way-weary men,
The clear beacon of God   bright in the heavens
Suddenly stop.   The star shone light
And white o'er the house   where for His will
Dwelt the Holy Bairn.   And the wife did keep Him,
The Maid most fittingly.   The minds, the hearts of the
                                            thanes
Became blithe in their breasts.   Through the beacon's
                            light they well understood
That they had indeed   found the Peace-Bairn of God,
The Holy King of the Heaven.   When they entered the house,
Did go with their gifts,   the great of the East,
The way-weary men —   quickly the warriors
Did know Him rightly, All-Wielding Christ.   In reverence
                                            now
They fell on their knees   before Him, the Child. In
                                    kingly wise
They greeted the Good One   and gave Him their gifts —
Gold and incense   as tokens of God,
And myrrh with it.   The men stood ready,
Fair before their Lord.   And with their hands all fit-
                                            tingly
They took Him and held Him.   They betook themselves
                                    then,
The wise men, into the house —   way-weary were they —
The sages into the guest hall.   There the angel of God
Did come to the sleepers,   showed a dream in the night,
Revealed in a vision,   as the Lord Himself,
The All-Wielder, did will it.   They thought a man had
                            commanded with words
That they seek them another way: the aethlings should
Leave and go to their own land   and not seek the loath-
                                    some man,
Herod, the mad-minded king.   Then morning did come
Shining down to the world.   The wise men began

To tell each other their dreams.   They did rightly
                              fathom
The All-Wielder's word.   For great wisdom
They bore in their breasts.   They bade the All-Wielder,
The Heaven-King on High,   that hencefore they might
                              still
Work His grace and His will;   quoth that their souls
                    were turned unto Him,
Their minds every morn.   Then the men travelled hence,
The earls from the East,   as the angel of God
Had told them with words.   They took them another way,
Following God's message.   Nor would they give
The king of the Jews   account of the birth of the Babe;
But as they did will it,   they went on their way,
The road-weary men, saying nothing.

IX

                    Soon after the Wielder's,
God's angel did come   and to Joseph did speak,
In a dream did say   to the sleeper at night —
The Master's own herald —   that the slime-mouthed
                              king
Would seek Him indeed,   the Child of God:
He was after His life.   "Now thou shalt lead Him
Out into Egypt-land,   live midst the land-folk
There with God's Bairn;   and with God's handmaid as well
Thou shalt dwell with the folk,   until unto thee cometh
The Word of the Master,   that thou mayest lead
The Holy Bairn, lead the Lord   back to this landscape."
Then from his dream Joseph   did waken, jump up
In his great hall.   God's orders
He soon recognized;   started out on his way,
The thane with the Maid.   Over the mighty mountains
He sought other folk.   For he wished to lead forth
God's Bairn from His foes.   Soon after the word
Came to Herod the king,   as he sat in his kingdom,

23

That the wise men   were gone from the West
Home to their Eastlands,   had fared on another way.
He knew that they had not wanted   to tell him the news
Here in his halls.   Then his heart was troubled,
His mind most mournful;   quoth that the men had done
                     this,
The heroes, to scorn him.   So he sat there sorrowed,
Bitter rage in his breast.   Quoth that a better idea,
Another he had now thought out.   "I know His age now,
Know His winters' number;   thus I can now bring it to
                     pass
That on this earth   He shall never grow old,
Here 'mid my hosts."   So Herod sent harshly
A command o'er his kingdom.   The king of the people
Hight his men go forth;   hight them behead with their
                     hand-strength
So many a babe,   bairns born in Bethlehem
And bred these two years.   The thanes of the king
Did evil deed.   So had to die there,
Though sinless, many a man-child.   Never since nor be-
                     fore
Such a pitiful killing   of young kin was there,
Such a wretched death!   The women wept.
Many mothers did see   their sons killed and dead;
Nor might they help them a whit,   with their two hands
                     hold them,
With their arms embrace them,   their own dear bairns,
Their loved and little ones.   But life it had to relin-
                     quish —
The babe in front of its mother.   Their misdeeds these
                     rogues
Saw not, saw not their sins.   With the sword's edge
They committed great crimes.   They cut down many
A child-young man.   The mothers bewailed
The death of their babes.   Care was in Bethlehem,
Loudest lamenting: if they had lashed
Their hearts with a sword's edge,   they could not have
                     hurt

Them worse in this world.   The women many,
The brides there of Bethlehem: they saw before them
                          their bairns,
The child-young men   lying murdered:
Bloody they lay on their laps.   The baneful murderers
Killed the innocent crowd.   From their crimes
They refrained not a whit: it was their will
To kill Christ Himself.   But God, strong and clever,
Saved Him from them   and their hatred. In the night
He had the earls   lead Him to Egypt-land,
The good men with Joseph   to the green fields,
To the richest earth,   where that river floweth,
The Nile-stream wide,   north to the sea,
The fairest of floods.   There the Peace-Bairn of God
Dwelled as He willed   until Weird did remove
Herod the King. Hate-filled,   forsook he the children
                          of men,
The life of the earth-folk.   O'er his lands
His heir was to rule.   Archilaus
He was hight, hero   of helm-wearers — he!
He was to rule o'er the Jewish folk   there in Jerusalem,
Wield power o'er the people.   Then the word did come
There in Egypt   to the aethling man:
That he spoke to Joseph —   God's angel himself,
The Lord God's herald.   Hight him again lead the Babe
Back to the land.   "Now he hath left the light,"
Quoth he, "Herod the king.   Once 'twas his will to kill
                          Him,
Delivering Him from this life.   Now in peace ye may lead
The Child to His kinsmen.   Now the king liveth not,
That insolent earl."   Joseph understood
God's token completely.   Straightway they readied
                          themselves,
The thane with the Maid.   They speedily sought to go
                          thence,
Both with the Bairn.   Bright fate they fulfilled,
The will of the Wielder,   as He bade them with words.

Mary and Joseph were again   come to Galilee-land;
The Holy Family   of the King of Heaven
Were with Him at Nazareth-burg.   There he waxed 'mid
            the folk,
Our saving Christ.   He grew full of sense, full of
            knowledge,
And the grace of God was with Him,   and great the love
Of His mother's kin: like no other man was He,
This Youth in His goodness.   When twelve years He did
            have,
When such an age He'd attained,   there the time was
            then come,
When they in Jerusalem,   the Jewish folk all,
Should serve their Lord,   their God Himself
And should work His will.   They were in the temple
There in Jerusalem,   the Jews all together,
Mighty gathering of men.   And Mary herself
Was there in the crowd;   and her Son she had with her,
God's Own Bairn. When they now   had made sacrifice goodly,
The earls at the altar,   as their law did order,
Had fulfilled their folk-way —   the folk fared thence,
The world-men as they willed it;   while in the temple
Stood God's Mighty Child,   though His mother most
            truly
Knew nothing of it.   Now, she weened He had left,
Had fared with her friends.   She first found it out
On the day that came after,   the aethling's wife,
The holy Maid — that He   was not 'mid the men-folk.
Then Mary's spirit   was deeply in sorrow,
Her heart most troubled,   that she did not find the Holy
            Child
Among the crowd.   Greatly she was grieved then,
The handmaid of God. She hied   herself to Jerusalem
            once more
To seek her Son.   And she found Him sitting

Inside the temple,   where sat the sages,
The very wise men   who verily read
And learned God's law,   how with their words
They could work the praise   of Him Who created this
                              world.
There sat in their midst   God's Mighty Bairn,
All-Wielding Christ —   although those who there warded
The temple could not   recognize Him even a whit.
And anxious for knowledge,   He asked them questions
With wise words indeed.   They wondered all
How so childlike a Man   could utter such speeches,
He with His mouth.   There His mother did find Him
Sitting down 'mongst the sages;   and she greeted her
                              Son,
The Wise 'mid the folk.   And with her words she did
                              speak:
"Why, dearest Man,   hast Thou given Thy mother
Such sorrow indeed,   that I needs must seek Thee —
I, worried wife,   a woman so troubled,
Among these burghers?"   Then answered the Bairn
With wise words, indeed: "What? Thou knowest right
                              well," quoth He,
"That I here belong;   with happiness here
Most rightly dwell   where My Mighty Father
Wieldeth His powers."   The woman understood not,
Nor the sages there in the temple,   why He said such a
                              word,
Did speak with His mouth   such a sentence. Mary kept
                              all
Concealed in her breast,   what she heard her Bairn speak
With His wise words.   Then they went from there,
Left Jerusalem both,   Mary and Joseph.
They had with them   the Son of the Lord,
The Best of all Bairns   that was ever born,
Child from a mother: they had for Him mighty love
With pureness of heart,   and He hearkened to them,
God's Own Bairn   to His blood-kin,

To His parents twain   through His humble mind.
In His childhood He never   sought to reveal
His greatness of strength,   that so mighty a power
He did have in this world;   but He bided His time —
In proper manner thirty years   in the midst of the people,
Before He would show   a single token,
Say to the people   that He Himself was
Here in this mid-world   the Master of Mankind.
To Himself He had kept it,   God's Holy Bairn —
The word and the wisdom   and all His great wit,
His very wise mind.   From His words no man would know,
From His speech,   that such wit was His —
That this Hero harbored such thoughts.   But as was
                              proper to Him,
He awaited the shining token: His time was not come
                              yet,
When He o'er this mid-world   should make it wide known,
Should teach the folk   to follow their belief
And to work God's will.   But many well knew,
Folk in the land,   that He was come to the light,
Though they could not recognize   Him all clearly as
                              yet,
Until He Himself   would indeed say the word.

XI

John had grown up   out of his earliest youth,
Had waxed in the wilderness.   Nor was there any world-
                              man
But him alone who so   served All-Wielding Christ.
Faithful His thane,   he forsook the multitude,
The company of men.   Then came to him mightily
There in the wilderness   word from Heaven:
God's goodly voice   gave John command
To proclaim Christ's coming,   proclaim His great
                              strength
Wide o'er this mid-world   with words of truth;

Hight that he say   that the true Kingdom of Heaven
Was close for them,   the children of mankind,
In this landscape here   was near for the land-folk,
The most wonderous riches.   His will was great
To relate to them   of such blessed raptures.
He set out and went   where the water,
The Jordan did flow   all joyfully there,
Made known through the land   to the landsmen all day,
To the folk that   with fasting they might atone
For many a wrong,   make better their sins themselves.
"That ye may now become clean," quoth he.   "The Heaven-
    ly Kingdom is close
For the children of men.   Ye yourselves in your minds
In your spirits, too,   rue all your sins, rue
The hurts ye have done against folk,   and hearken ye
    to my teachings,
Turn to my words.   Into the water
I shall dip you all dearly,   though from your deeds,
Your sins, though, themselves   I cannot absolve you —
That ye through my handwork   are henceforth cleansed
Of your loathsome deeds.   But He is come to this light,
Mighty to mankind,   and standeth right in your midst;
Though ye yourselves   do not want to see Him,
He will baptize you   both in the name of the Lord
And of the Holy Ghost.   He is Lord High over all.
He can free each man   from his misdeeds,
Shear him from sin,   who would be blessed of soul
Here in this world,   if such be his will:
To do what God's   Own Dear Bairn doth command
For these earth-folk here.   As His herald now
I am come to this world   and shall make Him His way,
Teaching the clansmen   to keep their belief
Through pureness of heart,   that they go not to hell
Nor face the fire.   Full glad be his soul then,
Joyous so many an hour —   whosoever forsaketh sin
And the devil's ambush: he acquireth the grace
Of the Good One, the Heaven-King —   he who hath a heart
    pure and loyal

For Almighty God."   Many an earl
Through these teachings,   many folk truly,
World-men did ween   that this was All-Wielding Christ,
Since he did so speak   so much of soothness,
Such words of truth.   Then wide and far it was known
To every man   over the promised land,
To all kin in their courtyards: then there did come
Jewish folk seeking him   out from Jerusalem,
Grooms from the bastions,   and asked if he were God's
                                    Bairn
"About whom so long," quoth they,   "the land-folk have
                                    spoken,
The world-men said verily,   that he should come to this
                                    world."
But John took the word   and boldly did speak
To the heralds. "I am not,"   quoth he, "God's Bairn,
The Verily Wielding Christ.   But I am here to make way
For Him, for my Lord."   The heroes then asked,
The earls who were hearing   asked the herald then;
Those from the town asked him for tidings.   "If thou are
                                    not truly God's Bairn,
Art thou then Elias,   who in earlier days
Was amid the folk?   Certainly he is again
Come on this mid-world.   Say what manner of man
Art thou? One of those   who was once here,
One of the soothsayers?   What shall we say
To the folk, tell them   of truth? Never was come
To this mid-world   another man ever
So famous of deed.   Why dost thou dip
These folk here,   if the foretold Savior
Thou art not?" Then John the Good   wisely gave answer:
"I am the foreboder, the envoy   of Him, of my Master,
My beloved God.   I am to make ready the land,
The world-folk right to His will.   Through His word in-
                                    deed
My voice is made strong,   though few understand it,
The world-folk here in the wilderness.   In no way am I
                                    like unto Him,

30

Like my Master and Lord.   He is mighty of deed,
Is so noble and strong —   that shall be soon known to
                                the many,
The war-men here in this world —   so that I am not worthy
Of tying the lace of His shoe,   though His own slave
I be — and He so lofty a Lord;   so much better
Is He than I.   No herald on earth
Is His equal now   nor ever shall be
On the face of this world.   Keep ye your will with Him,
O ye folk, your belief,   for long shall ye be
Then joyous of heart;   for the forces of hell
Ye have forsaken and the evils of life;   and seek ye then
                                for yourselves
God's light, home of   all heavenly good, eternal king-
                                dom,
High meadows of Heaven.   Nor let ye your hearts be in
                                doubt."

XII

So the young man told,   as were God's teachings,
Revelations to mankind.   Many did gather
In Bethany there,   the bairns of Israel —
Came there to John,   the king's underlings all,
People to learn,   and received belief.
He dipped them each day   and reproached them their deeds,
Their will to do wrong;   and for them praised God's Word,
The Word of his Lord: "The Heavenly Kingdom," quoth he,
"Standeth ready and right for all men   who are mindful
                                of God
And believe in the Healer   with pureness of heart,
And list to his teachings."   He was not long there,
That from Galilee came   God's Own Bairn,
Our Dear Lord's Son,   seeking to be dipped.
Our Good Wielder's Bairn   was now so grown
That among the land-folk   He had lived
Thirty winters here in this world.   As was His will,

He came there, when John   baptized them in Jordan's
                    stream,
Dipped the folk right dearly   and all day long.
Straightway when he saw   his Master Sweet,
His Lord, his heart grew blithe,   for that was his wish,
And with words he addressed Him: this goodly man, John,
                    spoke to Christ:
"Now Thou art come to my dipping,   my Lord, O my God,
Thou Best of Folk-Rulers.   So I shall do for Thee,
Since Thou art the strongest of kings."   Christ Himself
                    hight him,
The Wielder all verily,   that he utter such words no more.
"Knowest thou that it is fitting,"   quoth He   "that we now
                    fulfill
Forthwith all that is right,   as is truly His will?"
John stood and dipped   much folk all the day,
Many world-men in water;   and also All-Wielding Christ,
The High King of Heaven,   with his hands he baptized
In the best of baths;   and he bent his knee
To pray, strong as he was.   And Christ arose,
Fair from the flood,   Peace-Bairn of God,
The Lord of all Land-Folk.   When He entered the land,
Heavens door did ope,   and from the All-Wielder above
Came the Holy Ghost,   came down to the Christ.
He came in the likeness   of a lovely bird,
A strong, fair dove, and He sat Him down   upon our sweet
                    Lord's shoulder,
Hovered over the Wielder's Bairn.   Then word came from Heaven,
Loud from the high, cloudless vault,   and greeted the
                    Healer Himself,
Christ, the Best of All Kings.   Quoth that He Himself had
                    chosen
Him from His kingdom.   Quoth that He loved His Son
Best of all born men.   Quoth that He was His all-dearest
                    Bairn.
As God willed it for him,   John verily saw this
And heard it as well.   Soon after this he did make known

To the children of men   that they had a Mighty Lord,
"This is," quoth he,   "the Heaven-King's Son,
The One All-Wielder.   Of this I will be witness
Here in the world: for God's word did tell it,
The voice of my Lord,   when He hight me dip them,
The world-folk in water,   when I truly did see
The Holy Ghost mightily   coming down from Heaven's
                         meadows,
Seeking a single Man   in this mid-world here.
'That,' quoth that voice,   'that will be Christ,
The Fair Son of the Lord.   He shall dip the folk
In the Holy Ghost   and heal many a man
From his dire misdeeds.'   This power He doth have from
                         Lord God:
That He can remove   from all mankind
Their blame and their sins.   This is Christ Himself,
God's Own Bairn,   the Best of all Men,
Bulwark against the baleful fiend.   Well — ye may be
                         joyous of mind
Here in this world.   As it was your will,
While still alive,   to see your Land-Ward
Himself. Released from its sin,   many a soul,
Many a ghost will go   to his God, will be
Freed from his misdeeds,   which here toileth loyally
                         with friends
And firmly believeth   in All-Wielding Lord,
In Christ Himself.   That will be of great help,
Of goodly avail to all men,   whosoever gladly so do."

                         XIII

Then I found this to be: that to all folk,
To all peoples, John   praised Christ's teachings,
Those of his Lord,   through which they could win
The Kingdom of Heaven,   the holiest of goods,
Blessed life eternal.   But He Himself, our Lord so
                         good,

The Son of The Wielder   went in the wilderness
After the dipping.   He was there in the desert,
Our Lord of Earls,   a long, long while,
Nor had He more folk about Him,   more men in His follow-
                              ing.
He Himself chose it to be   even so.   He wished
To be tempted   by the most terrible of demons,
Strong Satan Himself,   who drives folk to sin,
Drives men to their misdeeds.   He knew Satan's mind,
The evil will of the varlet,   who once in this world
At its very beginning   betrayed them, the earth-folk,
Seduced them with sinfulness,   since he caused those two,
Partners in wedlock,   Adam and Eve, to become untrue
Through deceit — so that   the children of men
After their earth-trip   must travel to hell,
The ghosts of all folk.   This God Almighty —
All-Wielder, He — wanted to change;   He wanted to give
                     to the earth-folk all
The high realm of Heaven.   Therefore He sent here a Holy
                              Herald,
Sent His Son Himself.   Then Satan was filled
With hate in his heart.   He begrudged Heaven's kingdom
To the children of men.   He aimed to cheat Him, the Mighty,
Cheat the Son of the Lord   with the selfsame tricks
With which he had   once so treacherously
Gulled Adam himself,   so that he grew hateful to God —
He deceived Him with sin: the same he minded to do
To All-Healing Christ.   But He kept steadfast His heart
'Gainst the wicked wight —   the All-Wielder's Bairn
Kept hardened His heart.   He wished Heaven's kingdom
Secure for the land-folk.   The Land-Warden lay lonely
For forty nights.   He did fast there,
The Master of Mankind.   As long as He partook not of
                     meat,
Then they did not dare,   those devilish wights,
The hate-minded fiends,   fare nearer unto His face
Or greet Him. He weened   that *that* long He was truly as
                     God,

34

Unmixed with something   of mankind — the Mighty One
Heaven's Holy Warder.   As He let Himself hunger,
So that He began to want meat   because of His manliness,
There came closer the Fiend   after the forty days,
The murky misdoer.   He weened that surely He was simply
                    a man.
Then he went and spoke   unto Him with these words.
The spear-foe did greet Him: "If Thou art God's Son,"
                    quoth he,
"Why hast Thou not,   if Thou hast the power,
Ordered these stones to be bread,   and, Best of all Bairns,
Hast not healed Thyself of Thy hunger?"   Then spoke
                    again Holy Christ:
"The children of men," quoth He,   "may not live alone
By bread, the earth-folk all,   but they shall be
In this world for the teaching of God   and shall do the
                    works
Which have been proclaimed aloud   by the Holy Tongue,
The gums, the voice of Lord God: that is a good man's
                    life,
For the kinfolk all,   that they accomplish
What they are bidden   by the word of the Wielder."
The noisome fiend   came nearer then
For another time   and slyly tempted
And baited his Master.   The Peace-Bairn of God suffered
The will of the Evil One   and indeed gave him power
That he might try himself   against His great might.
He let him lead Him —   the scourge of the land-folk —
And take Him on to Jerusalem   there to the temple of God:
High over all   on the very highest of houses
He did set Him up   and spoke scorn-words to Him,
The Evil One with such mockery.   "If Thou art the Al-
                    mighty's Son,"
Quoth he, "glide down to earth.   Long hath it stood
Written in books   that He hath bidden —
The Almighty Father —   bidden His angels
That they be Thy warders   on all of Thy ways,

Hold Thee under their hands.   Why then? Thou mayest
                              never
Stub even Thy foot   on any hard stone."
Then spoke again Holy Christ,   the Best of all Bairns:
"So it is also most rightly   written in books," quoth
                              He,
"That thou shalt not try Him,   shalt not tempt Thy Master,
Thy Liege Lord ever.   That befits thee not in the least."
For a third time then He let   the scourge of the land-
                              folk
Take Him up high on a mountain.   There the treacherous
                              Fiend
Let Him look over   all of the land-folk,
Over winsome goods   and the worldly kingdoms
And all such possessions   as the earth surrounds
For fairer use. And there spoke   The Fiend once again
                              to Him,
Quoth that He would give unto Him   all those so goodly
                              things,
These noble fiefdoms,   "If Thou wilt kneel before me,
Fall in front of my feet,   confess me Thy lord,
And pray at my lap: then will I let Thee enjoy
All these possessions, which I have here placed before Thee."
No longer would He listen   to the loathsome word;
Holy Christ no longer would hear,   but He drove him
                              forth,
Away from His favor; swept Satan   away, and then spoke:
The Best of All Bairns   bade that men all should pray
To Almighty God;   and Him alone
Should they serve —   the many thanes,
The heroes hoping for grace,   "There help will reach
Every man whosoever he be."   Then the menace of men,
Satan himself became   saddened of mind;
The devil went down   to the dales of hell.
There came much folk from the Almighty   above down to Christ:
God's angels did come   to give unto Him
Friendship and following   and to serve Him faithfully,
                              humbly,

36

As one should one's God, one's Liege,   the King of Heaven
                Himself, for His grace.

For a long while then, God's Blessed Bairn   dwelt in
                the wilderness,
Till it seemed to Him better   for the benefit of all
That He show His great strength   to the folk. Thus He
                forsook
The shade of the forest, the spot in the wood,
And again He did seek   the company of earls,
The illustrious thanes   and the throngs of men,
And He betook Himself to Jordan's shore.   There John
                found Him,
The Peace-Bairn of God,   his Master all good,
The Holy Heaven-King.   And he said to the Hero,
John, His disciple,   when he saw Him coming:
"That is the Lamb of God,   who shall release the folk
In this wide, wide world   from their wicked sins,
All men from their misdeeds: glorious Master,
Most Strong of All Kings!"   Christ then went forth
To Galilee-land,   God's Own Bairn
Fared to His Friends,   where fair He was born
And most rightly reared;   and related with words,
Christ 'mongst His kinfolk,   the Richest of Kings,
How they themselves should   atone for their sins;
Hight them to rue   their harmful works many,
To let fall their false deeds: "Now 'tis fulfilled,
As the old men have said,   as the sages did speak,
Promised help unto you   from the Heavenly Kingdom.
Now it is near through the Savior's strength.   And ye
                shall rejoice therein,
Each of you will gladly   give service to God
And will work His will."   There arose joy 'mid the world-
                folk,
'Mid the gathered crowd.   Christ's teachings became
                sweet

To the followers all. He began   to gather together
Youths for disciples,   young men and good,
Word-wise warriors.   He went to the shores of a water,
There where the Jordan   had spread to a sea
On the border of Galilee-land.   There He saw sitting
Andrew and Peter, found the two   by the flowing water.
The brothers both   down by the broad stream
Were very neatly   throwing their nets,
Fishing in the flood.   There first the Peace Bairn of
                    God
Himself did greet them   on the shores of the sea.
Hight that they follow Him,   quoth that He would give
                    them
Much of God's kingdom.   "As ye here catch fish,
So shall ye both with the force of your hands   fetch the
                    children of men,
So that they may enter   the Kingdom of Heaven,
People aplenty through your message and word."   Much
                    pleased of spirit were they,
Both of the brothers.   They perceived God's Bairn,
Their beloved Lord.   They left all things,
Andrew and Peter, whatever they owned by the flood,
Had won by the water.   Truly the will was great in them
To go along   with the Bairn of God,
To be in His retinue   and to reap blessed reward.
So do all folk   who would earn their Lord's favor
And would work His will.   As they went along
The shores of the water,   they met a sage
Sitting by the sea   and his sons twain,
Jacob and John,   young men on the Jordan.
Sons and father,   they sat on the sands;
Neatly they knotted   and mended their nets
With both their hands, the nets   which the night before
They had slit in the sea.   Then He spoke unto them;
God's Blessed Bairn bade them   be on their way now with
                    Him.
Jacob and John,   they both did go,

The child-young men.   Christ's word was for them
So worthy here in this world,   that on the shores of
                    the water
They forsook their father   alone by the flood,
The ancient alone,   and all that they owned,
Their nets and their well nailed ships.   They chose
                    All-Nurturing Christ,
Holy Savior and Lord.   To earn His help
Was the need they felt.   So feel all thanes,
All warriors here in this world.   Then the All-Wielder's
                    Son
Went forth with the four.   And He chose the fifth;
Christ picked at a market place   a king's young vassal,
A wise-minded man: Matthew was he hight.
A thane was he   to an aethling-born.
There he was to take   with his hands tithe and toll
For his lord;   loyal he was to his task,
Noble his looks and his bearing.   But he left them all —
Gold and silver   and gifts so many,
Treasures most dear —   and became our Lord's man.
The king's thane chose   Christ for his Lord,
A more generous Gift-Giver   than ever his master
Had been in this world.   He received a worthier thing,
Longer lasting gains.   It became known to the land-
                    folk,
To each in his bastion,   that the Bairn of God
Was gathering disciples,   and He Himself spoke
So many a wise word   and such words of truth,
That shining wonders   He did show them and tokens
Did work in this world.   Through His works
It was visible, through His deeds as well,   that He
                    was the Master,
The Heavenly Lord   who had come to help
The children of men   in this mid-world here —
The land-folk toward light.

To the land He oft made this clear;
For He worked there   so many a wonderous token,
As He healed with His hands   the halt and the blind,
Relieved many land-folk   from loathsome ills,
From such sickness   as at that time Fiend Satan
Had thrown on the children of men —   the hardest of
                              all,
Long lasting illness.   The land-folk came there
Day after day,   where our Dear Lord was
Himself with His faithful,   until many folk
Were gathered together,   a very great crowd
Of land-folk, though they were not   all come with a
                              like belief,
World-men all with one will: some sought the All-
                              Wielder's Bairn —
Poor men were they   and in want of food —
So that they might beg Him   amid the multitude
For meat and for drink, amid the crowd;   for there was
                              many
A goodly thane   who gladly did give
Of his alms to the poor.   And again there were some,
Clans of the Jews, sly folk were they.   They were come
                              to this place,
So that they might discover   our Master's deeds
And His words as well.   Stealthy of mind were they,
Wrathful of will. They wanted   to make All-Wielding
                              Christ
Loathed by all land-folk.   Thus would they not list
To His teachings nor turn to His will.   Some others
                              were sages,
Wise men indeed   and worthy of God:
Among the people the pious.   They were come for the
                              preaching of Christ,
So that they might hear   the Holy Word
And learn and listen.   Their belief they had firmly
                              established —

They had pious hearts;   and straightway they became
His thanes,
So that on the day of their death   He would take them
to the dearest of goods —
The Kingdom of Heaven.   Christ gladly received
So many of mankind and granted unto them   His merci-
ful rule
For a long, long time —   for that so well He could do.
There was a great crowd   gathered round glorious
Christ:
So much of the folk was assembled.   He saw them come
from all lands,
From all the wide ways,   the world-men together,
Fine folk and strong.   His fame was spread far
To many a man.   Then the Mighty Christ
Went up on a mountain,   the Mightiest of Bairn;
And He sat aside from the rest.   There He chose for
Himself
Twelve specially picked,   men true and loyal —
Good folk whom He wished   with Him as His vassals,
Disciples of Him,   their Master, each day.
He called them by name   and bade them come nearer:
First surely Andrew   and Peter also,
The brothers twain,   and these two with them,
Jacob and John —   they were worthy of God.
Mildly inclined was His mind unto them.   They were one
man's sons
Both through their birth.   The Bairn of God chose them,
These fair ones, as followers;   and much folk, too,
Most famous men: Matthew and Thomas,
The Judases twain   and the other Jacob;
He was a cousin of His —   they were come from two sis-
ters,
Come from the same clan,   Christ and Jacob, very good
kin.
Now All-Healing Christ   counted nine of His men,
Loyal hearted thanes they.   Then He hight the tenth
also come

And join His disciples: Simon was he called.
And He called Bartholomew, too,   to fare up the mountain
Away from the folk.   And Philip was with them.
True hearted men were they all.   The twelve went to-
                                gether,
The fighters all to the confab,   there where the Coun-
                                cillor sat;
The Protector of Many   made known unto them
How He planned to help mankind   'gainst the pangs of
                                hell,
'Gainst the infernal flame —   help those who would
                                follow
The fair, sweet message,   as He sought to reveal it
There in His wisdom   to the world-folk many.

                        X V I

Then they stepped nearer   to All-Saving Christ,
Such disciples,   as He had chosen Himself,
The Wielder amid His vassals there.   And the wise men
The heroes, stood all gladly   about God's Son,
The war-men most willingly;   they awaited His word,
Thought and were silent, longing to hear   what the
                                Lord of the Land-folk,
The Wielder Himself,   would make known with His words
For love of the land-folk.   There sat the Shepherd of
                                Lands
Across from his good men,   God's Own Bairn.
With His talk 'twas His will   to teach them — the people —
Wise words aplenty: how in the realms of this world
They could best bring about   bounteous praise of our
                                Lord.
He sat there, was silent —   our Holy Savior —
And looked at them long.   Our Lord was gracious of
                                spirit,
Mild was His mood;   and as He unlocked His mouth,
The All-Wielder's Son   did show them with words

42

Many a marvelous thing;   and to the men He said
Such wise words — to them, whom   He, All-Wielding Christ
Had chosen here for this speech: those of the children
                    of earth
Who were worthiest of God,   men of good clan.
He spoke to them soothly;   and said those were blessed,
The men on the mid-earth,   who in their minds,
Their hearts, were poor for humility's sake.   "For to
                    them is given
The Eternal Kingdom, the holiest   of Heaven's meadows,
Life without end."   And He also told them,
That blessed were, too, the gentle and mild.   "They may
                    inherit this glorious earth,
The very same kingdom."   Quoth that those, too, were
                    blessed
Who bemoan here their misdeeds.   "Await joy they may,
Consolation perfect   in their Master's kingdom.
Blessed be those who have done good,   heroes who justly
                    have judged:
For their piety they will   be plenteously filled
In the kingdom of God: such good things will greet
                    them,
These world-men who have judged   well and justly.   Nor
                    will they be cheated
In secret, when they sit at the confab.   Blessed be also
                    such men
Whose hearts are mild in their heroes' breasts.   For them
                    will the Holy Lord,
The Mighty, be mild.   Blessed those 'mid the folk
Who have cleaned their hearts: They will see the
                    Heaven-Wielder
In His own kingdom."   Quoth that they, too, were
                    blessed
Who live in peace 'mid the folk.   "Have started no feud,
                    no affair,
With their doing. Sons of the Lord   indeed they'll be
                    called.

For He Himself will be gracious to them,   Most gladly
                    will they
Long enjoy the Lord's kingdom."   Quoth that they, too,
                    were blessed,
Those war-men who ever will right,   "and through this
                    willingly suffer
The harm and hatred of richer men.   To them is the
                    Meadow
Of God's Heaven then given,   and the spirit's good life
Forever, for all days,   and the end never cometh
Of the winsome possessions."   So All-Wielding Christ
Had told the earls 'round about Him   of eight blessed states;
Through these shall each one straightway   find Heaven,
                    if that be his wish;
Or he shall be deprived   of joy and possession
For eternal times,   as soon as he exits this world,
Life's fate on this earth,   and seeketh another light,
Either a fair one or a foul —   even as he hath lived
                    'mid the folk,
Worked with them here in the world.   Thus He spoke with
                    His words.
All-Wielding Christ,   the Richest of Kings,
The Own Bairn of God   did say to His disciples;
"Ye shall also become blessed,"   quoth He, "because
                    the people,
The folk of the land   will fight you, speak evil of
                    you all,
Hold you up to scorn   and harm you muchly
Here in this world;   and working worse wrong,
Condemn you with sinful speech   and so much of hatred;
Denying your teachings   and doing loathsome deeds,
Harm for your Lord's sake.   But let ye your hearts still
                    be happy,
Your lives ever, too, since reward   standeth ready for
                    you
In the kingdom of God;   and every good, also,
Great and manifold: that is given unto you as a gift,

44

A treasure, since here first   ye have toiled, have en-
                         dured
Pain in this world.   It is worse for those others:
Grimmer judgment awaits them   who have goods here on
                         earth,
Wide worldly treasure.   They waste here their pleasure,
Enjoy them enough.   These men shall suffer
A harrowing judgment   after their journey.
They shall bemoan their misery,   who are now so merry
And living in lust,   nor let go willingly
Their sinful thoughts,   which tempt their spirits,
Their loathsome wrongs.   For them shall come as reward
An evil most painful. These people   will see sadly
                         their plight,
Face troubled their end.   All sore shall their spirits
                         be,
For too much in this world   they followed their will,
These men, as they were minded, indeed.   Now for their
                         misdeeds ye shall
Reproach them, rise against them with words,   as I now
                         shall reveal unto you
And most soothly say,   O ye, My disciples,
With words of truth: that of this world
Ye shall henceforth be the salt   of sinful mankind,
Absolve them from bad deeds,   so that to a better thing
They may turn the land-folk: to forsaking the Fiend's
                         work,
The deeds of the devil;   and to seeking their dear Lord's
                         realm.
So with your lessons   ye shall turn the land-folk
To My will. However,   if any of you fade away,
Turn aside from the teachings   which are entrusted to
                         you,
Then ye are like unto salt   which is scattered
Wide on the seashore;   then it is of worth to none,
And the bairns of the land-folk   will walk on it with
                         their feet,

Men grind it in grit.   All who are to proclaim it, God's
                                    Word,
Will thus suffer: if he permiteth his spirit to doubt,
If he is not bent to spur   men to the blithe realm of
                                    Heaven,
But wavereth in his word —   then the Wielder groweth
                                    grim,
The Almighty is enraged,   and the children of men, also.
To the bairns of the earth   he will become hated,
To all the land-folk,   if his lesson be not of worth."

XVII

So spoke He wisely   and said God's spell.
The Land-Warder taught them, His people   with pureness
                                    of mind.
The heroes stood gladly   'round the Son of God,
World-men to His will.   They longed for His words;
They thought and were silent.   They heard Him say it —
The Lord of the Land-folk   give God's law to the children
                                    of men:
He promised them Heaven   and thus spoke to the heroes:
This, too, I may tell you,   My disciples, most truly
With soothy words: that ye henceforth shall be
The light in this world   to the bairns of the lands-
                                    men,
Friend to all people   and over much folk,
Shining and winsome: nor may your great works
Remain hidden, nor yet   with what hearts ye proclaim
                                    them —
No more than a castle   can remain ever concealed
Which standeth on a mountain   or steep on a cliff,
A giant-made work.   No more can your words
In this mid-world, your deeds be hidden to men.   Do as
                                    I teach you:
Let your light shine forth   large to the land-folk,
To the bairns of men,   that they may know your minds
                                    and your souls,

46

Your words and your will,   and thus praise All-Wielding
                    God,
Their Father in Heaven,   with pureness of heart;
Here in this light praise Him   who gave this lesson to
                    you.
Let him who hath light   leave it not hidden from the
                    land-folk,
Nor cover it heavily;   rather high in his great hall
He shall set it up,   so that all within shall have sight
                    thereof,
The heroes in the great hall.   Even so may ye not hide
The Holy Word from the folk   here in this land,
Keeping it from man's kind;   but the commandment of
                    God
Ye shall spread abroad   so that all the bairns
Over this large landscape,   the folk shall indeed un-
                    derstand.
And so do ye   that which in former days
The wisest men   did speak with their words,
When they then, the earls,   did follow the old law,
And for this reason as well,   as I now say unto you:
That all men may serve God   as the old law doth bid
                    them.
Never ween for one instant   that I come to this world
To lay low and destroy   the old law
Among the people, or to contradict   the word of the
                    prophets,
Who, as men of truth,   gave clear commandments
In days of yore.   Sooner shall both fall apart,
Heaven and earth,   which are held bound together,
Before any word   which verily the wise men
Commanded the folk   remaineth one whit unfulfilled
Here in this light.   I came not to World
That I should fell it, the prophets' word,   but to ful-
                    fill it rather —
To enlarge it and make it anew   for the aethling bairns,
For the good of this folk.   That was formerly written

In the old law: ye have oft heard it spoken
By word-wise men: whosoever doth act thusly here in
                                        this world,
That he berefts another   of his old years,
Whosoever cheats him of life: to him shall the children
                                        of men
Deal out death; and now   I shall tell you more deeply,
Shall discuss it still further: whosoever shall fos-
                                        ter hatred,
One man 'gainst another,   deep in his mind —
Who beareth a grudge in his breast,   though they be
                                        all brothers,
God's blessed folk,   bound together in kinship,
Men into clans. And still a one   becometh so grim of
                                        mood
'Gainst the other, that he would rob him of life,   if
                                        he could right well do it,
Then he is straightway doomed —   deprived of *his*
                                        life,
Is indeed so judged,   as was the other
Who through the might of his hands   cut off the head
Of another earl.   Also in the law it is written
With words of truth: and ye all know it well —
That with all one's heart   one should love one's
                                        neighbor,
Most zealously love those closest,   be kind to one's
                                        kinsmen,
Good to all kith,   and mild in one's gift-giving;
Have love for his friends   and hate for his foes,
Withstand them with a strong,   with a strife-eager
                                        heart,
Ready 'gainst their evil and wrath.   But I relate yet
                                        another law,
A fuller one still for the folk: that ye have fondness
                                        now for your foe,
In your heart love him well   as ye would your kin —
And in God's name ye so do it.   Do ye much good unto
                                        him,

48

Show him pureness of spirit   and loyalty sweet;
In return for his loathsomeness do ye love him. That
                              is long lasting counsel
For every man   whose mind hath been turned
In hate 'gainst his foe.   Ye shall all gain from this,
For ye shall be called   the Heaven King's sons,
His bairns all blithe.   Nor may ye find better counsel
Anywhere here in this world.   I verily tell unto you,
Say to each bairn,   that ye may not bring
Your goods with an angry heart   into God's temple,
Into the Wielder's house: it be not worthy
For Him to accept,   as long as ye harbor anger,
Foster fiendishness, one to another,   far deep in
                              your hearts.
First shalt thou be reconciled   with him who opposeth
                              thee,
Shalt be tranquil of spirit;   then mayest thou offer
                        thy treasures,
On God's altar give them —   worthy they be of our good
                              Lord,
Of the Heaven King worthy. For His kindness shall ye
                        serve Him more,
For His favor follow God's will more,   than most of
                        the other Jews do,
If ye would someday own   the Eternal Kingdom,
See life without end.   I shall still say unto you,
As the old law   once bade you:
An earl should never covet   another man's wife,
Seduce her with sin.   This I also say unto you now,
Soothy words: that a man's eye   may quickly lead him
                              astray
Into murky misdeeds,   if he letteth his mind be driven,
So that he beginneth to yearn for her   who may never
                              be his.
Then he hath straightway   done sin unto himself,
Hath loaded hell-pangs   upon his heart.
If then a man's eye   or again his right hand

Or some limb lead him   along the loathsome way,
Then 'twould indeed be   better for yon earl,
Better for that bairn of men,   that from his body he
                    loose it,
Cast it from him afar,   coming to Heaven without it —
Than that he flee with all   to Inferno,
That with a whole body he go   to the grounds of hell.
Human frailty so willeth,   that no man shall follow his
                    friend,
Though a dear friend he be,   if he driveth him on to
                    sin,
Draweth him down to guilt. 'Tis no matter then,   how
                close they do stand in the
                    clan,
How mighty their kinship,   if he maketh him murder,
Draweth him down to misdeeds.   Better he do this:
That he cast his friend   far away from him
And lose all his kinsmen   and have no love for a one,
That he may alone   mount on high
To the kingdom of Heaven,   than in the pangs of hell
Both would suffer   broad punishments, too,
And horrible pain.

XVIII

Here in the law it also
Standeth written with soothy words,   so that ye may all
                understand it:
That all people should ever   avoid perjury,
Nor themselves swear falsely,   since that is great sin,
Leading much folk astray   along loathsome ways.
Then I shall also say unto you,   that no one should
                    swear,
No child of man swear   any such oath,
Neither by Heaven on high   (since that is the Lord's
                    throne)
Nor by the earth here below   (since that is All-Wielder's

Footstool so fair),   nor should any child of the folk
Swear by his own head,   since he may turn not a single
                            hair,
Either black or white,   but as Holy God
Hath mightily marked it.   Therefore the many,
The earls should avoid   every oath-word. He who oft
Sweareth becometh steadily worse,   since no longer
                        can he ward for himself.
Therefore I say unto you   with soothy words
That ye shall never swear   any stronger oaths,
Mightier ones with men   except as with My words
I most verily here   do command you:
If a man hath trouble with another, let him speak the
                            truth;
Say 'yea,' if it be so,   confess that it is true;
Say 'nay,' if it be not,   and let that be enough.
If a man sayeth more,   much beyond that,
It becometh a bad thing   for the bairns of men,
So that earls, all disloyal,   will not believe
One another's word.   Then I also verily tell unto you:
As by the old law   you were so bidden:
Whosoever taketh   the eye of another man,
Looseneth it from his body,   or some limb indeed —
That he shall pay   to the person for the loss
With a like limb of his own.   Now I give you this lesson:
Ye shall not wreak vengeance   for deeds done wrong.
Instead shall ye suffer most humbly   all things your-
                            selves,
The pain and the wrong   that people will do you here
                        in this world.
Let each earl do unto another   whatsoever is good and
                        is useful,
If he so willeth,   that the children of men
Do good unto him;   that God will be mild unto him,
Mild unto each man   who doeth the Master's will.
Respect ye the poor   and divide ye your riches,
Among those who are needy. Nor be ye troubled,   if ye
                        receive no thanks,

No reward in this passing world.   But well may ye hope
That your Dear Master,   your Mighty Liege,
Will reward you with gifts,   grant you good pay
For what ye have done   for your love of Him.
If thou wouldest give   to good men all
Fair shining coins,   and thinkest thereby
To reap a reward,   how willest thou then have return
                                       from God,
Or largess here in the light?   For these are brief-
                                       lasting goods.
So it is for all   that thou doest for others,
For love of the land-folk —   if thou thinkest to re-
                                       ceive the like
In word and in work: why should the Wielder know
                                       thanks,
Since thou givest to them   and gettest from them in
                                       return?
Give thou thy riches   to the poor men, who give unto
                                       thee
No rewards in this world;   and strive then for the
                                       Wielder's realm.
But act thou not loudly,   when thou givest thy alms
To the needy of men;   but be thou meek all of mind,
Glad for God's thanks;   for a goodly reward wilt thou
                                       take,
Find a fair return,   where far longer
Thou shalt use it.   That which thou   givest with a
                                       pious heart,
And sharest in secret,   is esteemed by our Lord.
Nor boast of thy giving —   let no great lord do so
                                       either —
Lest through idle boasts   the gift is made nought
And forlornly lost.   Before the eyes of the Lord
Shalt thou receive thy reward   for thy work right
                                       and good.
Also shall I bid thee,   when thou bendest thy knee
In prayer, begging help   from the Lord, begging

That He grant thee release   from the loathsome thing,
From sin and from shame,   which ye yourselves
Have wrongfully wrought —   ask not before others
Nor make it known to the many,   lest men extol you
And give praise unto you;   and the prayer to your Lord
You lose most forlornly   for idle fame.
But if ye do ask help   from your Lord on high,
Praying most humbly to Him —   that must ye surely here
                    do —
That your Battle-Lord   befree you from sin,
Do ye so in the darkness: yet your Lord doth know,
He, Holy in Heaven,   since nothing is hidden to Him,
Neither of words nor of works.   Thus will He make it,
As ye have bidden of Him —   if unto Him ye have bent
Your knee, your hearts being pure."   The heroes all
                    rose,
The men stood gladly   around God's Son,
The world-men to their will.   They longed for such
                    words,
Pondered and kept their peace.   The people had need
To think over again   all that the Holy Bairn
Had told unto them   on this first time,
Had all clearly proclaimed.   Then spoke one of the
                    twelve;
Of the goodly men one began   to ask of God's Bairn:

XIX

"Master good," quoth he,   "we are in need of Thy grace
To work Thy will   and Thy word as well,
Best of All Bairns,   and we bid Thee teach us
To pray, Thy disciples,   as doeth John,
The dear Baptist,   on every day,
Teaching his world-folk with words   how to greet the
                    Wielder,
To speak to their God.   For Thy disciples   do Thou the
                    same.

Reveal Thou the runes."   Then the Ruler had ready
His answer for them,   the Son of the Lord,
For them His good word.   "If ye would greet God,"
                    quoth He,
"With your words   greet the Wielder,
The King Full of Strength,   speak ye then as I teach
                    you:
Father of us,   who art all Thy folk-bairns,
Thou who art on high   in the kingdom of Heaven,
Hallowed Thy name   here in every world,
Thy kingdom come   in strength and craft,
Thy will be done   over all the world;
As here on earth;   so there above
On high in the   kingdom of Heaven.
Give us each day, good Lord,   Thy gracious guidance,
Thy holy help, and absolve us,   O Warder of Heaven,
From the manifold mischief   we do against mankind,
Let not loathsome wights   lead us astray,
As is their will   and as we are worthy;
But help us against   all our evil deeds.
So shall ye bid Him,   when ye bend for prayer,
Ye men, with your words,   that the Mighty Wielder
Release you from the loathsomeness   that is in all
                    land-folk,
If ye then would forgive   the land-folk all
Of their sins and their selfishness,   such wrongs as
                    they
Have done against you —   The Great Wielding God will
                    absolve you,
The Father forgive you   your frequent faults
And your heavy sins.   But if ye harden your hearts,
Are not willed to absolve other earls,   other men from
                    their wrong,
Then Almighty God will not forgive   you your grim sins,
But ye shall receive   from Him just reward,
Payment most pain-filled   throughout plenteous time,
For all the unrightness   ye have done against others

In the light of this world, without that ye have
willed
To make peace in your matters with the children of
men
Before ye shall wander, O ye men, out of this world.
Today I shall also tell you how ye shall bring My
teachings to pass:
For if ye would indeed keep a fast
To make little your misdeeds, make it not known
To the many, but hide it from all; yet Almighty God
knoweth well,
The Wielder, your will; if other world-bairns,
Other land-folk fail to laud you, yet lovely reward
He will give,
Your Holy Father, in Heaven's kingdom,
Since ye have served Him, ye men, so humbly here,
So piously all 'mid the people. Unright possessions,
O my earls, covet them not; but care for rewards above
With All-Wielding God. That is a weightier thing
Than if a man liveth richly here on this earth,
Winning the goods of this world. If ye would hear then
My word,
Gather ye not great treasures, neither silver nor gold
In this mid-world here, nor hoards of riches;
For it reddens with rust here, and robbers will steal it.
Worms gnaw it away; the garments wear threadbare,
The gold-wealth is gone. Do ye good works
And gather in Heaven a hoard far greater,
Riches fairer by far. Your foe cannot rob you,
Can take nothing from you. For treasures stand ready
For you up yonder, as much as ye there
Have gathered in Heaven riches and goods,
Heroes, ye, through your hand-gifts. And keep ye stead-
fast your hearts
For this; for there lie the thoughts of men,
Their minds and their hearts; there lieth the hoard,
The goods all gathered. Nor is any man so greatly
blessed,

That both he may do   in this broad, wide world:
That on this earth   he may live richly indeed
In all of his world-lusts,   yet thankfully serve All-
                    Wielding God
At the selfsame time: but he shall ever
Forsake wholly one   or the other,
Either the lusts of the body   or life everlasting.
Therefore grieve ye not for your garments,   but hold ye
                    fast unto God,
Nor mourn in your minds,   how on the morrow
Ye may find eat and drink,   or, ye aethlings,
What weeds ye will wear;   for All-Wielding God
Knoweth the needs of them   who now serve Him well,
Following the will of their Liege.   Why, by the winged
                    birds
Ye may verily see it: they that are in this world
Flitting about in their feather-dress.   Though they
                    have won no fortune,
Yet the Lord, our God,   giveth to them each day
Help against hunger.   Ye may in your hearts
Eke gaze at the flowers,   when ye think of your gar-
                    ments,
How fairly they are garbed,   as they stand in the
                    field
Brightly blowing.   Nor did that warder of bastions,
Solomon the King,   who had costlier treasure,
Greater gold-hoards   than any had e'er gained,
Had won more wealth,   the choicest of weeds —
Still in this life,   though he was lord of these lands
                    all —
He never found raiment as fair   as this flower hath
                    on,
Which here in the field   standeth ready and fair,
Lily with so lovely a bloom.   The Wielder of Lands
                    hath so garbed it
From the high fields of Heaven.   But this folk is far
                    dearer,

The men mean far more,   those whom He hath made in
                    this land,
Wielding o'er them, as He willed.   Therefore may ye
            not worry concerning your
                    dress,
Grieve over your garments so much;   God will give
                counsel,
Help from Heaven's meadow,   if ye willingly serve for
                His favor,
Always yearn for God's kingdom;   then act ye according
            to those, His good works.
Strive ye for right things.   Then will our Rich Lord
Gift you with all goods indeed,   if ye so willingly
                    go,
Following Him, as I tell unto you   with soothy words.

xx

Ye shall never speak an unjust,   a wrong judgment
Over any man,   or accuse him falsely;
For doom falleth over him,   so that the cares full
                    well,
The worries wax large   of him who did speak such words
Of wrong against others.   Not a one of you
Shall give wrong measure   to another man,
Being feloniously bent   in buying or selling
While on this earth here;   for to each earl will hap
Even as he hath done unto others —   even there where
                he would dearly
Not see his sins.   Eke must I say yet unto you
Where ye must guard   against the greatest of evils,
Against wrong-doings many: Why wilt thou reproach
                    a man?
He is thy brother.   Thou seest under his brow
A wisp in his eye,   but are not willing by one whit
To think of the beam   which thou hast in thy own,
A hard tree and heavy.   Into thy heart let it

First fall: how to remove it.   Then wilt thy light
                        shine forth,
Thine eyen will be opened.   Thus mayest thou later
Make better the sight   of thy sweet friend,
Heal it, lo, in his head.   Let each in his heart,
Each man in this mid-world,   think more of his own
                        misdeeds
Than he thinketh   of the sins of another,
The faults of a friend —   and hath himself done far
                        worse,
Far greater wrongs.   If to himself he would do good,
Then shall he first make himself   free of all sin,
Loose of all loathsome deeds.   Later may he then with
                        his teachings
Be a help to the people,   when he knoweth himself to
                        be pure
And safe from sin.   Nor shalt thou strew
Thy sea-pearls down before swine,   nor scatter thy
                        jewels,
Nor thy neckband holy;   for they will trample it now
                        in the mire,
Besmirch it in sand.   For they know nothing,   the swine,
                        of cleanness,
Of sea-pearls so fair.   Here there are many such folk
Who will not hear   thy holy word
Nor follow God's teachings,   and know of no good.
They would far liefer   have low, useless things,
Have empty words,   than the work and the will
Of your Wielder and God.   They are not worthy,
That they hear your holy word.   For in their hearts
                        they do not think,
Do not want to learn it nor do it.   Say ye nought of
                        your words unto them,
Lest ye squander God's speech   and many a spell.
Lose ye not your word 'mid the land-folk,   who do not
                        want to believe it,
The great and true word.   Eke shall ye guard against

58

The wiles of this folk,   as ye wander, ye earls, through
the land,
Lest the teachers of lies   lead you astray
With words and with works.   They come wearing such
garbs,
To you wearing fairer jewels: but their hearts are wily.
They speak wise words,   but their works are worth nought,
The thoughts of these thanes.   For ye know that thorns
never grow
On the wineberry   nor on that which is worthy,
On the fairer fruits.   Nor does a man gather figs
From the hawthorn tree.   Keep ye this truth in your
hearts:
That the bad tree   which standeth there in the earth
Never giveth forth good fruit;   and that God hath not
shaped it,
That the good tree of the bairns   of men bear bitter
fruit;
But from every tree whatsoever   there cometh forth
only
Such fruit to this world   as was born from the root,
Either bright fruit or bitter.   That is the feeling
in the breasts,
In the hearts of so many   of the kinfolk of man,
Wherever each one of the earls   showeth himself all
openly,
Maketh known with his mouth   of what mind he is,
The thoughts in his heart;   nor may he hide them ever;
But from an evil man   cometh unwise counsel,
Words bitter and blameworthy,   such as he hath in his
breast,
Harboring them 'round his heart: here his thoughts
become known,
His will along with his words;   and his works follow,
too.
There cometh from a good man   an answer, gracious and
clear,

Wise in his wit,   that he ever speaketh with words —
The man with his mouth;   such words as he hath in his
                              mind,
Hoarded round his heart.   Thence cometh the Holy Gospel,
That most Winsome Word,   and his works shall thrive
For the good of men,   for many a thane,
As indeed is his will,   even as the Wielder
Did grant unto good men,   God Almighty,
The High Liege of Heaven,   since without His will
Neither with words nor with works   can they do one
                              whit
Of good in this world-garden here.   Therefore all the
              bairns of mankind should most gladly
Believe in the strength   and the might of this One
                   Single Lord.

                        XXI

Here I must tell you, too   that pathways twain
Lie in this light.   Thereon the land-bairns
Must travel, the children of earth.   One of the twain
Is a street broad and wide: much folk wandereth on it,
Of mankind so many;   for their mind doth drive them —
The world-lust, these war-men.   On the worse side
It doth lead them, the landsmen,   where they are lost,
The heroes in hell fire;   there it is swarthy and hot,
Horrible within. Easily   may the children of earth
Travel thereto. Still in the end   it availeth them
                   not.
Then lieth again another   and narrower path,
A way in this world,   on which do wander
But few of the folk.   The bairns of men follow it
Ungladly, though it goeth   on to God's kingdom,
Leadeth all aethlings   into eternal life.
But take ye the narrow one;   though it be never so
                   easy
For world-folk to wander on, it availeth well

Whosoever trespasseth it;   he hath bounteous pay,
Long-lasting reward   and life never ending,
The dearest of doing.   And do ye so pray
To your Lord, the Wielder,   that this be the way
Ye follow forthwith,   and going further along this
                        path
Into God's realm.   For He is ready ever
To give in return,   if a man biddeth rightly,
If the folk-bairns do ask him.   Seek ye your Father,
Which is in the kingdom unending.   There can ye find
                        Him
For your welfare eternal.   Make ye known your travels
At your Master's door;   for you they may open,
Heaven's portals unlock,   so that to the holy light,
To God's realm itself,   now ye may go,
Seeing life everlasting.   Lo, I shall say unto you,
Tell you one token more   truly for the earth-folk all,
That every man whosoever   keepeth My teachings
Held in his heart,   who thinketh of them in his mind,
And worketh them in this world —   he worketh indeed
Like a wise man   having great wit,
A head that is clearer.   And he chooseth his homestead
On right fast ground,   and upon a rock
He worketh the walls,   where neither the wind
Nor the wave nor the water's stream   can harm it a
                        whit,
But it standeth there   strong 'gainst all storms
High on the rock,   since right firmly it was
Set on the stone. From beneath,   the spot holds it
                        steady,
True and straight 'gainst the wind,   that it cannot
                        topple.
Thus doeth each man,   who willeth not
To hear these, my teachings,   or to carry them out:
He acteth indeed   like the unwise earl,
Like the witless world-man,   who on the water's shore,
On the sand itself,   would set up his great halled
                        house,

Where the western wind   and the waves of the stream,
The tides of the sea do tear it,   sand and grit cannot
Hold it up 'gainst the flood,   since it stood not fast,
Firmly timbered in earth.   So shall the work of each
                                        earl
Strive for this, each aethling   who followeth My Word,
Holdeth My holy commandments."   In their hearts they
                                        began,
The many children of men, to wonder: they heard the
                                Almighty God's
Love-filled lessons.   In this land they were truly
                                not wont
To hear such things   being said ever before,
Either of words or of works.   But wise men understood,
That He so taught unto them   words of great truth,
The Liege of the Land-folk,   since He, lo, had power
Unlike unto others,   who in earlier days
Were chosen to teach   from the children of men
From the clans themselves.   Never had of Christ's words
The like been heard 'mid the land-folk,   when He set
                                down His law
To the bairns on the mountain.

XXII

            He bade them do both:
Not only should they say   and spread His word,
How one should reach   the realms of Heaven,
The Farspreading Fiefdom;   but first He did lend
Unto them the power to heal   the halt and the blind,
The ills of the world-folk,   their manifold weakness
And terrible plagues;   and He bade them, too,
Never to garner money   from any man
Or to take treasured pay.   To them He did tell this:
"Keep ye well in mind, how this wit   and this wisdom
                        were come unto you,
And the Father of all Folk hath lent you   the force. Ye
                        need not buy it

With goods nor pay for it with gold.   Therefore be ye
                    gracious unto men;
Mild in your hearts   and ready to help,
Teaching the land-bairns   long-lasting counsel,
Enduring deeds.   Deal ye right heavily still with
                    their wrongs,
With their swarthy sins.   Let not silver nor gold
Be of such worth unto you,   that ye would e'er own
                    them,
Fair glimmering gold-pieces;   for they will give you
                    no joy,
Be useless to you.   Ye shall own no more garments,
My earls, no more weeds,   than those which ye wear,
Ye good men, to garb you,   when ye do go forth
Among the many.   Ye shall not think of your meat,
Not long of your body's food;   for the folk shall feed
Them that are teaching.   That shall be of use,
Which ye say to the folk —   of right fair reward.
Worthy is the workman,   that he be fed well,
The man given meat,   who shall care for so many,
The souls of the folk,   making firm the way
For the ghosts to God's meadow.   That is a greater
                    thing,
That a man should make ready   for the souls of the
                    many,
Should keep them all   for the kingdom of Heaven,
Than that he careth   for the bodies of folk
With meat, for the children of men.   Therefore should
                    mankind
Keep fondly and sweetly   those who show them
The way to Heaven's kingdom   and hold the harm-doer,
The Fiend far from them;   who give them blame for
                    their faults,
For their sins dire and swarthy.   Now I shall send you
Throughout the landscape,   like a lamb among wolves.
So shall ye fare 'mid the foe,   amid world-folk many,
Amid unlike men.   Keep ye your minds toward them

So clear and clever   as the bright-colored worm,
The slyly wise serpent,   when it doth suspect
A deadly foe.   Then men of the folk
Cannot lead you astray.   Ye shall take care
Lest men turn away   the thoughts of your mind
And destroy your will.   Be ye wary of them,
Of their furtive deeds   again like the dove;
Having toward all folk   a simple heart,
Meekness of mind,   so that no man can be cheated,
Be ever deceived   by your deeds,
Led astray by your sins.   Now shall ye fare
On your way with these tidings: much toil shall ye
                                   bear
Amid the people   and oppression together,
Much and varied,   if in My name
Ye do teach the land-folk.   Ye shall yet receive much
                                   of evil
From the people of world   and still worse pain
For this, My right word;   before the kingdoms of World
Shall ye oft stand bound   and suffer both
Mockery and scornful speech: but let not your spirits
                                   feel doubt,
Nor your souls ever err;   nor need ye ever
Harbor care in your heart —   when they call ye forth
                                   from the crowd,
Bid you go with them   to the guest hall —
What ye will say unto them   with your good words,
How ye will speak to them wisely;   for success will
                                   come unto you,
Help come from Heaven,   and the Holy Ghost will speak
Mightily out of your mouth.   Therefore dread ye not
                                   the hatred of men,
Fear not their fiendishness.   For though they have power
Over your life, may rob   your body of breath,
Slay you with swords —   yet not a whit of your soul
Can they e'er destroy.   Dread ye All-Wielding God,
Fear ye your Father.   For Him gladly

64

Do ye His commandment,   for He hath might and power
Over both, o'er the life of a man,   o'er his body as
                              well,
Yea, even o'er the soul itself.   If for the sake of
                    these teachings
Ye lose your life on the way,   then in the light of
                              God
Ye shall find it again,   for the Father,
The Holy Lord God, hath kept it   in the kingdom of
                              Heaven.

XXIII

Not all will reach Heaven   who here hail Me Protector,
Their Master and Lord.   There are many of them
Who willingly kneel   to the Liege every day,
Calling on Him for help,   but have other thoughts in
                    their hearts,
Working dastardly deeds;   they win no gain from their
                              words.
But those may hasten   toward Heaven's light,
Go on to the kingdom of God,   who gladly here
Accomplish the work of the Wielder,   and His will
                    as well.
They need not call unto Him, their Master,   with words
                    so many,
Hailing Him for help,   since All-Holy God,
Knoweth of every man   the thoughts in his mind,
His word and his will,   and payeth him right for his
                              work.
As ye fare on your way,   let this be your worry
And your task as well: to fulfill my tidings,
As ye fare on your path,   far o'er the landscape
Through the wideness of world,   where your ways will
                    lead you,
The broad street to the borough: straightway seek
                    ye the best

Men among the multitude,   and make ye known unto
                                them
With words of truth what lieth in your minds.   If they
                          be worthy
Of this: that they gladly give   help to your good works
With pureness of heart,   then may ye dwell in the
                                house
With them as ye will,   rewarding them well:
Pay them with goodness —   give them to God Himself
With your words, foretelling   the Wielder's sure peace,
The holy help   of the King of Heaven.
Yet if they cannot   become blessed
By their own deeds,   cannot do your works,
Carry out your message: then leave ye these men,
Fare forth from this folk;   and your peace will fare
                          forth with you
Once more on the very same way;   and leave ye them in
                          their wickedness,
In their works of sin,   and seek for yourselves another
                                way,
A much larger gathering;   nor leave ye of dust one
                          single grain
To follow your feet from there,   where one hath re-
                          ceived you unfairly;
But shake ye that dust from your shoes,   so that it
                          becometh a shame,
A witness there to the world-folk,   that their work
                          is worth nought.
Then I tell unto you and in truth: that when this
                          world doth come to its end
And that Famous Day   fareth over all mankind,
That the city of Sodom,   which for its sins
Was felled to its fundament   by the force of the
                                flame,
The power of fire —   it will have more peace,
A milder protector   than shall have those men
Who cast you aside, were unwilling   to accomplish your
                                word.

Whosoever receiveth you   with a pious soul
And mildness of mind,   he hath done so for Me,
Hath accomplished My will,   accepted All-Wielding God,
Your Mighty Father,   Master of Mankind,
The Rich Giver of Truth,   who knoweth all right.
The Wielder Himself doth know   and reward the work
Of each earthling,   if to any man ever
He doeth some good   for the love of God:
Willingly giveth   water to drink
That the needy man   is healed of his thirst
From the cold well-spring.   The word will come true.
It will never fail,   that he find fair
Reward in the eyes of God,   receive recompense
Of many a sort for that   which he doeth in God's sweet
                    love.
But whosoever of the bairns of men   doth deny Me here,
Of the warriors before the host,   in Heaven I shall
                    likewise do unto him
Far above before the All-Wielding Father   and before the
                    strength of His angels,
Before their multitude.   Whosoever of the children of
                    men
Doth not with his words   deny Me here in this world,
But before the kinship of men   confesses he is My
                    disciple,
Him will I vouch for   before God's very eyen,
Before the Father of All,   there where so many folk
Wend their way   to the All-Wielder
To justify their deeds   before the Great Judge.
                    There will I be,
As is meet, a mild Protector   for whosoever hearkeneth
                    unto Me,
Who hath heard My word,   and accomplished the work,
Which I have commanded of you   up here on the mountain."
So the Son of the Wielder   verily taught the world-
                    folk
How they should work God's love.   Then He sent them
                    away,

The men of His host,   each to his own home.
They had heard the Word,   the Heaven King's holy
                              Spell.
Whosoever in this world was wiser   in word and in
                              deed,
Many of mankind   over the face of this mid-world,
Smarter in speech —   he heard the Spell
Which the Richest of Men   spoke on the mountain.

XXIV

It was three nights later,   that the Lord of the
                              Land-folk
Went into Galilee-land   there to a wedding feast:
God's Bairn had been bidden.   A bride would be given,
A most lovely maid.   Mary was there,
The Mighty One's mother.   The Lord of the Many,
God's Own Bairn, did   go with His followers
To the high house,   where the hordes were drinking,
The Jews in the guest-hall.   He did go to the feast,
Made known to the guests,   that He had God's power,
Help from the Heaven-Father   and the Holy Ghost,
The All-Wielder's wisdom.   The warriors were blithe,
The land-folk together   loud in their joy,
Glad-hearted the guests.   The grooms went about
Pouring from pitchers;   the pure wine they
Carried in jugs and in cups.   The crowd's tumult
Was gay in the great hall,   when the folk began, one
                              'mid the other,
To feel their best blitheness;   there on the benches
In rapture were they,   when the wine ran out,
The fruit drink of the folk —   for nought was there
                              left,
No drop in the house,   which to the hordes
The butlers might bear,   when all of the vessels
Were empty of mead.   'Twas not long after that
That the fairest of ladies   did find this out,

The mother of Christ.   She went to speak to her Kin,
To her Son Himself;   she said with her words
That the host of the house   had no more of wine,
Hight the Holy Christ,   that He find some help
For the joy of the many.   There again God's Mighty
                                     Bairn
Had ready His word: with His mother He spoke:
"What doth the mead of these men,"   quoth He, "mean
                              to Me,
The wine of this world-folk?   Why, O goodwife, speaketh
                              thou
So much, admonishing Me   before these many?
My time is not come yet!"   Yet she still trusted well
Deep in her heart,   the Holy Maid,
That the Wielder's Bairn —   even after these words —
Would help indeed,   the Best of All Healers.
Then the sweetest of ladies   hight all the servants,
The butlers and cup-bearers   who had here been serving,
That they omit not a whit   either of words or of works
Of that which the Holy Christ   would hight them do
For the people there.   The pots all stood empty,
Stone vessels six.   Quite softly He bade them —
God's Mighty Bairn —   so that many a man
Was verily all unaware   what He said with His words.
He hight that the butlers   should fill the barrels,
The cup-bearers there, with clearest water;   with His
                              fingers He blessed it,
With His hands turned it to wine;   and He hight the
                              vessels be filled,
The pitchers be poured from;   and He spoke to the
                              servants,
Hight that they give with their hands   to the foremost
                              guest
Who was here at the feast: for him pour a fulsome jug,
Who next to the host was the noblest there.   When he
                              now drank the wine,
He was loathe to keep still;   but before the many he
                              spake

To the bridegroom then;   quoth that the best mead
                    should have been brought,
The finest of the fruit-wines   given first to the
                    earls
At once at the wedding.   "So is a man's wit
Awakened by the wine,   and he waxeth blithe,
Maketh merry with drink.   Then mayest thou bring on
The worser wines.   That is the way of this folk.
But most strangely indeed   hast thou marked thy host-
                    ship
Among the multitude here;   thou hast hight thy serv-
                    ing men,
Thy butlers and cup-bearers   bring out at the ban-
                    quet
Of all the wines   the very worst forsooth,
Serving that first at the feast.   Now that thy guests
                    are filled,
The dear banqueteers   are already most drunk,
The folk feeling merry,   thou hightest brought forth
The loveliest of all wines   which I ever saw lifted
Anywhere in this earth-light.   Thou shouldst have
                    given that earlier,
Have served us sooner.   Such thanks wouldst thou then
Have garnered from all the good men."   Many a thane
                    grew
Aware after these words —   as soon as they had drunk
                    of the wine —
That here in the house   the Holy Christ
Had revealed a token.   They trusted thereafter
The more in His rule: that He had God's might
To wield in this world.   So it came widely known
Over Galilee-land   to the Jewish folk
That the Son of the Lord   had Himself turned
The water to wine.   That was of His wonders
The first which He showed   as a sign to the Jewish
                    folk,
As a token in Galilee-land.   Nor may anyone tell

70

Nor say forsooth,   what hath happed since then
In the way of wonders among the folk;   for All-Wielding
                    Christ
Told His teachings   unto the people of Jews
The livelong day   in the name of Lord God,
Promised the kingdom of Heaven;   with His words pro-
                    tected them, too,
From the press of hell.   Hight that they should seek
                    the wardship of God
And eternal life.   There is the light of the souls,
The Lord's life ever joyous,   the glow of the day,
The good glory of God.   There many guests
Dwell to His will,   who here have thought well
How best they should keep it,   the Heaven-King's
                    commandment.

                    XXV

With His followers   He went forth from the feast,
Christ to Capernaum,   the Richest of Kings,
To that famous town.   Much folk was assembled,
Was gathered around Him,   men of good stock —
A blessed following it was.   They wanted to hear His
                    word,
Which was sweet and holy.   There came toward Him a
                    centurion;
A good man, he approached Him   and bade Him most
                    earnestly,
That the Holy One help him.   Quoth that at home
He had long had   a man lame and sickly,
In his family a feeble one,   "For I tell Thee no one
Can heal him with hands.   Now I have need of Thy help,
Good Lord, my Liege."   Then spoke the Peace-Bairn
                    of God
And straightway Himself   did say unto him,
Quoth that He would come   and save his young kin
From his direst need.   Then came nearer

The man from the multitude   to speak to the Mighty
          Christ,
To exchange words with Him.   "I am not worthy,"
          quoth he,
"Good Lord, my Liege,   that Thou wouldst come to
          my house —
Wouldst seek out my dwelling,   for I am a sinful man
With my words and my works.   I believe Thou wieldest
          might,
Canst work his healing   here in this place,
My Wielder and Lord;   if Thou speakest Thy word,
He is cured of his sickness;   clean and bright shining
Doth his body become,   if Thou wilt but give him Thy
          help.
I am a man holding office   and have wealth enough,
Have gained goodly things;   though I stand governed
By an aethling king,   yet have I of earls quite a
          following,
Loyal warriors in arms,   who listen alone unto me,
Who leave of word or of work   not a whit undone
Of that which I bid them   do here in the land;
But they fare forth and finish it,   do return to their
          master,
Being obedient to me, their lord.   Though I do own
          broad
Spreading goods in my house,   have servants enough,
War-minded men,   still may I not dare
To bid Thee, God's Bairn so Holy,   to enter my
          building,
To seek out my dwelling,   since I am so sinful,
So mindful, my Lord, of my misdeeds."   Then spoke once
          more All-Wielding Christ,
The Finest of Men, to His followers;   quoth that
          never had He found
Anywhere 'mongst the Jews,   among the offspring of
          Israel,
The like of this man   in the landscape;   one who be-
          lieved

More deeply in God, more purely   in Heaven — "Now may
Ye hear, ye too, what I say at this time   with words
                   of truth:
That much foreign folk   from the East and the West,
Many clans of mankind   shall come together,
God's holy folk   in the Heavenly Kingdom:
They will rest right well   in the lap of Abraham,
Of Isaac himself and of Jacob,   good men all, and
                   enjoy
Goods and good will   and a winsome life
And the great light with God.   But lo, many Jews,
The sons of this realm   will then be robbed,
Be sundered from such splendor,   and shall have to
                   lie
In the darkest dales   in the farthest distance of
                   all.
There one can hear   the heroes lamenting
And gnashing their teeth   in terror and pain.
There is furious rage   and a hungry fire
And the hard pangs of hell,   hot and thirsty,
Swarthy might, never ending,   as payment for sin,
For wretched wrong-doing,   to all who have not willed
                   to rid
Themselves of their wrongs   before they relinquish the
                   light,
Wend their way from this world.   Now if 'tis thy will,
Thou mayest go home.   In thy house thou wilt find
                   hale
And sound the child-young man: he will be joyous of
                   mind.
The bairn hath been healed;   even so as thou badest Me,
All hath been done,   even as thou hast belief
Firm fixed in thy heart."   Then to the Heaven-King,
To the All-Wielding Child of God   the centurion gave
                   thanks
Before all the folk for this,   that He had helped him
               thus in his anguish.

It was all worked,   even as he had wished it
And most blessed indeed: he did go on his way,
Went as he willed,   where he had ownership,
A house and a home.   There he found hale his bairn,
The child-young man. Christ's word   was accomplished,
                for He had
The might to show forth tokens,   so that no man could tell,
Over the earth could reckon,   that He through His
                own power,
Through His strength had made miracles   on this mid-
                world here,
Accomplished such marvels.   For all things stand in
                His might,
Both Heaven and earth.

XXVI

        Then the Holy Christ bethought Him
To fare on farther.   For the bairns of the folk
The Master of All,   the Almighty, the Good,
Every day did accomplish   deeds dear and good;
With words taught God's will   to the people, had always
Followers aplenty about Him,   blessed folk of God,
A mighty crowd of men,   come from many peoples,
A holy army and host.   He was good in His help,
Mild to the men.   Then He came with the many:
Now the Bairn of God   with a noisy crowd came to Nain,
The Savior to the high-standing   city. There His name
Would become famed among men.   There mightily
The Saving Christ walked along   until He came closer,
The Best of All Healers.   They saw folk bringing a
                body —
They came carrying   a corpse without life.
On a bier they bore it   through the gates of the
                bastion,
A child-young man.   The mother did follow,
Her heart being heavy;   herself did she beat with her
                hands,

74

Bewailed and lamented   the death of her bairn —
Unhappy woman was she —   it was her only child.
She was a widow,   in this world had no joy
Except this one son,   whom Weird had now taken.
She had lost all things,   had lost joy and happiness;
And now fate, ill-famed, had robbed her of him.   Many
                    people did follow,
A crowd of the burghers,   as they carried the bier,
The young man to his grave.   There the Son of God,
The Mighty grew mild;   and to the mother He spoke;
Hight the widow   leave off with her weeping,
Nor care for her child;   "Thou shalt see here the
                    strength,
The work of the Wielder: thy will shall be granted
                    thee,
Comfort in front of the folk: from now on thy spirit
May not bemoan thy bairn."   Then He went to the bier,
He Himself did touch it,   the Son of the Lord,
With His holy hands   and to the hero He spoke,
Hight this child, all too young,   to stand up, hight
                    him
Arise from his rest.   Right away the youth
Did sit up, the bairn on the bier;   and into his
                    breast came
His soul through the strength of God;   and he spoke
                    unto them,
The man to his kith.   Christ commended him then to
                    his mother,
The Holy One into her hands.   Her heart was consoled,
Happy the woman, since to her   so much grace had happed.
She fell to Christ's feet   and praised Him, the Folk-
                    Lord,
Master, before all the multitude,   since He had here
                    helped
Her loved one to live 'gainst the working of Weird.
                    Well she knew that He was
The Mighty Lord, the Holy, who governed the Heaven,
                    who could help so many

Of earthlings all.   Then many began to attend
The wonder, which had come to pass   there 'mid the folk:
              quoth that The Wielder Himself,
The Mighty, had come to teach them,   the many, that He
                    had sent
A prophet, most wonderous, to the kingdom of world;   one
                    who did His will.
Then truly many an earl   was taken by terror,
The folk full of fear,   for they saw him again
Alive and seeing the light of day;   him whom death had
                    but lately taken,
Stretched low on his sick-bed.   Again he was sound,
The young kin quickened;   and soon this did spread
To the heirs of all Israel.   And when evening came,
There were gathered about   many sick men together,
The halt and the lame of hand —   whosoever was here
And lived 'mid the land-folk;   they were led to the
                    place,
Were come to the Christ,   who through His strength and
                    His craft
Helped them and healed them   and sent them hale from
                    the place
To wend where they willed.   Therefore should one praise
                    His words,
The Mighty Minder   of all mankind,
Of whatsoever land-folk   verily believeth
In His word and His work.

XXVII

                    There were come so many
From all the foreign folk   for the glory of Christ,
For His mighty guardianship.   There onto a sea God's
                    Son
Wished to go with His vassals —   'twas on Galilee's
                    borders —
The Wielder onto a wave-tide.   There He willed that
                    the other folk

Go wandering ahead,   and He went with a few
Into a small ship,   the Savior Christ,
Way-weary, to sleep.   The weather-wise men
Raised high the sail,   let the wind drive the sloop
Over the sea-tide,   until they did come to the center,
The Wielder there with His vassals.   There began the
                    force of the weather;
The storm-wind rose,   the waves   waxed high,
Swarthy clouds swung down in between: the sea was
                    astir,
Wind battled water;   the men were worried.
The sea was so angry,   not a man expected
To live any longer.   The Land-Warden they then
Awakened with their words.   They told unto Him of the
                    weather's strength;
They bade saving Christ   to be gracious and kind, to help
'Gainst the waters.   "Else will we die,
Martyred here in the sea."   Then the Good Son of God
Arose, Himself from His sleep.   To His disciples He
                    spoke,
Bade them not to dread   the weather's battle one bit.
"Why art ye so fearful?" quoth He.   "Are your hearts
                    not yet firm,
Your belief yet so little.   'Twill not be long now
Then the stream shall   become stiller
And the weather all winsome."   Then He spoke to the
                    wind,
And to the sea itself.   And He said unto them
Both, that they should grow still.   And they hearkened
                    to His bidding,
To the Wielder's word.   The weather grew calm,
The flood became fair.   There the folk around Him,
The world-men did wonder,   and with their words some
                    did speak
What a Mighty One   this Man was indeed,
That the wind and the wave   would heed His word,
Both doing His bidding.   The Bairn of God

Had there saved them from need.   The sloop sailed on
                         farther,
The high-horned ship.   The heroes did come,
The leaders, to land.   They all lauded God
And praised His great power.   Then many people did
                         come
To the Son of God.   He received them most gladly,
Whosoever sought help   with a clear, pure heart.
He did teach them to believe,   and lo, their bodies
He healed with His hands;   though a man were hard
And piteously pressed   with plagues through Satan's
Wily followers,   though the force of the Fiend
Held him fast in his hands,   had destroyed his heart
And his wit as well,   that he went about
Mad among mankind;   yet Mighty Christ always,
The Healer, gave him back his life,   if he were come
                         to His hands,
Drove the devils hence   with the power of God,
With words of truth,   and returned him his wit,
Let him be healed   against the haters,
Gave him peace 'gainst the foe;   and they went forth,
Each into his own land,   whichever he loved the most.

                         XXVIII

So our Dear Lord's Son   did on each day
God's work with His followers.   But the Jews had no
                         faith,
Believed not at all   in the largeness of His strength:
That He was the All-Wielder   over all things,
Of lands and of people.   Their reward is still lasting:
'Tis farflung exile,   since they acted so evilly
'Gainst the Lord's Son Himself.   With His retainers He
                         soon went
Again into Galilee-land;   He did go with His friends,
God's own Bairn,   to where He was born,
Where as a young child   He had waxed with His kin,

78

He, the Healer All Holy.   Around Him a host,
A great crowd did throng.   There was many a thane
So blessed 'mid the crowd.   There some carried a sick
                                  man,
Certain earls in their arms.   Before Christ's eyen
                              they would
Bring him, before God's Bairn.   Betterment he needed,
Needed Heaven's Wielder   to heal him indeed,
The Minder of Men.   For many a day
He had been lamed of limb.   Little could he
Govern his body at all.   There were such great numbers
That they could not bring him   before God's Bairn,
Could not press through the people   to tell Him the
                                        plight
Of this poor, sick man.   There He hied Himself within,
To the hall, All Healing Christ —   a great crowd was
                              around Him,
A multitude of mankind.   There the men who had so long
Carried with them   the weak-limbed cripple
Began to speak how they might bear him   on the bed be-
                              fore God's Bairn,
Through the world-folk within, , so that Wielding Christ
Would see him Himself.   So his servants went,
With their hands they did lift him,   climbed high on
                              the house,
Slit open the hall from the roof   above, and with
                              ropes
Let him down in the building   where the Rich Lord was,
The Strongest of Kings.   When He saw him coming
Through the house's rafters,   right well He knew from
                              the hearts,
From the minds of these men,   that mighty indeed
Was their faith in Him.   And so spoke He before all
                              the folk,
Quoth that He would absolve   the sick man from sin.
In answer to this   the people did speak,
Rage-hardened Jews, quoth   how could it be so:

God alone can forgive   works of crime,
The world's All-Wielder.   His word He had ready,
God's Mighty Bairn.   "I make manifest,"   quoth He, "in
                                    this man
Who lieth so ill   here in this large hall —
Most grievously pained —   that I have the power
To forgive the sins   and to heal the sick man
Without even touching   My hand to him."
Then our Mighty Lord   admonished the man
Who lay there lame   to rise there before the land-folk,
To stand up hale.   And He hight him take on his shoulders,
On his back his bedding;   and he did our Lord's bidding,
Straightway before the assemblage,   and went away sound,
Hale from the house.   Then many a heathen,
Many a world-man did wonder,   quoth that the Wielder
                                    Himself,
Surely God the Almighty   had given unto Him
More splendid might   than unto any man's son,
The skill and the strength;   still they would not ac-
                                    knowledge,
That folk of the Jews,   that He was God,
Nor believed they His lesson,   but struggled evilly
                                    with Him,
Fought against His word.   For this they have won weary
                                    care,
Reaped a grievous return;   and right long will that last
For those who hear not   the Heaven-King's teachings,
The lesson of Christ,   which is proclaimed over all,
Wide and far in the world;   and He let them all see
                                    His work,
Each day and every   look on His deeds,
Hear His holy word,   which He spoke for the help
Of the bairns of mankind.   And so many and mighty
A token He showed,   that they trusted Him better,
Believed in His word.   So many a body
He unbound from ills baleful   and granted them better-
                                    ment,

Gave life to those destined   to die, even if
The hero was on hell's path already.   The Healer Him-
                    self did so —
Christ through His might and His power   quickened even
                    the dead after death,
Let them further enjoy   the winsomeness here in the
                    world.

XXIX

So healed He the halt   and the lame of hand,
Made better the blind,   let them see the bright light,
See Heaven's splendor;   absolved them from sin,
The world-men from wickedness.   But the Jews grew no
                    better,
This loathsome land-folk,   in their belief
In the Holy Christ;   but they were hardened of heart,
Strove very strongly against Him,   wanted not to perceive
They were well ensnared   by the devil's will,
This folk through its faith;   for He was not idle,
The Son of the Lord;   but with His words He said unto
                    them
How they could gain   the kingdom of Heaven;
And through all the land He did teach;   a multitude He
                    did turn
Unto Him with His words,   so that many a world-man,
A great crowd of folk, did follow Him.   And in figures
God's Bairn spoke unto them   things which in their
                    breast they could not perceive
Nor grasp in their hearts,   till the Holy Christ
With open words   willed to speak
To all people   through His power and strength,
And make clear what He meant.   A mighty crowd,
A very large one, thronged 'round Him.   They longed
                    greatly
To hear the true word   of the King of Heaven.
On the shores of the sea   by the water He stood.

Because of the great crowd,   He cared not to proclaim
His lesson to His thanes   there on the land;
But the Good One did go —   and His disciples with Him
             all gladly —
The Peace-Bairn of God   did go to a water
Unto a ship, hight   that it shove off
Further from the land   so that the folk,
The crowd, could not throng   quite so close. Many
                        a thane,
Much world-folk stood by the water,   where All-Wielding
                        Christ
Did reveal His lesson   to the land-folk there.
"Lo, I may say unto you,"   quoth He, "My disciples,
How an earl began   to sow good grain
In the soil with his hands.   Some fell on hard stones
From above, and the grains   had not earth enough
In which to grow rightly   and send down roots,
To sprout and cleave fast.   And that corn was lost,
That lay on those rocks.   Some fell on the land,
On excellent soil.   This soon began
To wax winsomely tall   and take root right well;
And most merrily it grew.   The land was so good,
So fruitful its kind.   Again, some had fallen
On a stiff, hard street,   where steps did tread,
The hoofbeats of horses   and the feet of heroes.
There was soil for them   and indeed they sprouted,
Began to wax on the way,   but the walking of men did
                        kill them,
The wayfaring of folk;   and the flying birds picked
                        them up,
So that they were   not one whit of use
To the owner there,   those that did fall on the way.
Some fell on that day   where there stood so many
Thickets of thorn.   There was soil there for them,
And they came up, they sprouted   and cleaved; but
                        weeds
Came between and kept them   from growing. The cover

Of forest spread out before them,   and they could not
                    grow fruitful,
Since the thornbrush   thronged all around them."
Christ's disciples did sit   and were silent all,
The word-wise thanes.   For they wondered muchly
With what goodly pictures   the Bairn of God
Would begin to say   such a true and wise spell.
Then one of the earls   began to ask
The Beloved Lord,   bent low before Him
Most humbly indeed.   "Why," quoth he, "Thou hast might
Both in Heaven and on earth,   Holy Master,
Above and beneath.   Beest Thou All-Wielder
Over the souls of men,   and we Thy disciples,
Given to Thee with all our hearts,   O Lord most Good.
If that be Thy will,   let us hear Thy good word,
That we can proclaim it   to all Christian folk.
We know indeed   that upon Thy words
Follow true parables;   and a need, most great, is in
                    us,
That in this land,   here with Thee, we may teach
Thy word and Thy work —   since from such wisdom it
                    cometh."

                    xxx

Then the Best of All Men   spoke in answer to them.
"I did not mean," quoth He,   "to disguise My deeds
In any way, either my words   or my works; but ye
                    shall know all,
Ye disciples Mine;   for unto you hath He granted,
The Wielder of Worlds,   that ye may well know
In your hearts and your minds   the mysteries of
                    Heaven.
Yet one must give unto others   the commandments of
                    God
With pictures in words.   Now will I tell you
Most truly what I mean indeed,   so that ye may better

Understand my teachings   over all the landscape.
The seed which I spoke of   is the Word of Himself,
The Holy Scripture   of the King of Heaven,
As one should spread it   o'er the mid-earth here,
Wide in this world.   World-folk, at heart,
Men are most different;   some are of such mind,
So hard of spirit   and evil of heart,
That it seemeth not worth their while   to act by
                    your words
Or to be so willed   to accomplish My teachings;
But My lessons all   are indeed lost unto them,
And the commandments of God   and the teachings of
                    you, My men,
On these evil folk;   as I earlier said unto you,
That the corn did wither,   which could not there
Strike root with its sprouts   upon the stones.
So all will be lost,   the speech of the aethling,
The message of God —   whatsoever one telleth
To an evil man;   and he chooseth the path,
The way on the left,   on the worse hand to God's dis-
                    pleasure,
To the foe of the folk   and the onslaught of fire
And the devil's joy.   From that day on
He shall heat the broad flames   with the heart in
                    his breast.
Nonetheless in this land   shall ye spread My lesson,
Proclaim it with words,   if there be many people,
Such earls on this earth.   Yet another man still may
                    exist
Who is young and clever   and hath kindness of heart,
Is wise in his speech,   understandeth your spell,
Pondereth it in his heart   and heareth it with his
                    ears
Very zealouly indeed;   and stepping closer,
Accepteth in his heart   the bidding of God,
Learning and carrying it out.   If his belief is so
                    good,

84

He will then wonder how he can woo another,
A wrong-doing man; so that his mind be filled
With a loyalty clear for the King of Heaven.
The bidding of God groweth broad in his bosom,
The willing belief, even as on the land
The grain doeth with its sprouts, when it hath right
ground,
Good soil to suit it, and the changing of weather —
The rain and the sun, so that it hath its right.
So doeth the teaching of God in a good-souled man
Through the day and night; and the devil stayeth far,
The wicked wight; and the word of God
Is nearer to him in the nights and the days,
So that it causeth him to accomplish both —
This lesson is a blessing to the bairns of the land —
That which cometh from his mouth, and the man becometh
of God.
So hath he bought with his heart in this hour of world
A piece of Heaven's kingdom, the greatest possession.
Into God's power he fareth, freed from wrong deeds.
Faithfulness
Is so good for each man. No treasure of gold
Is like unto belief. Henceforth teach ye the lesson
Mildly to mankind. These are so varied of mind,
The heroes of men; some have hard strife,
An evil will and a wavering spirit.
They are full of deceptions and deeds of wrong.
As one beginneth to think, as he standeth there
Among the crowd, and harkeneth with great care
To the teachings of God; then he thinketh he would
gladly
Henceforth carry them out. Then the teachings of God
Begin to cleave to his heart, until there come once
more
Through his hands possessions and proud wealth of
others;
Then loathsome wights lead him astray,

And avarice doth   seize him again
And killeth now his belief: thus was it little use
                    unto him
That he ever thought in his heart,   if he willed not
                    hold it.
Even so is the waxing   which began on the wayside,
Grew fair on the land; there the footsteps   of folk
                    could destroy it again.
So mighty sins   in the soul of that man
Do unto God's teachings,   if he take not heed.
Otherwise will they follow him   down far to the bottom,
To the heart of hell.   To the King of Heaven
He is of no further help,   but the Fiend
Will punish him direly with pain.   Likewise repair
                    ye forth,
Teaching with words in the world;   I will know the
                    hearts of the folk,
Many differences of mind   among mankind,
Their varied ways...[1]
Some have turned their spirits   entirely to this
And come more to keep their hoard   than to work the
                    Heaven King's
Will down on earth.   Therefore it waxeth not —
God's holy commandment —   though it may cleave there
And send forth roots.   But riches do crowd it,
Even as the weeds and the thorn   entangle the corn
And keep it from waxing: so doeth wealth to a man.
He fettereth his heart   so that he here pondereth not,
The man in his mind,   what he needeth most:
How he will work that indeed   as long as he liveth here
                    in this world,
That he have Heaven's Kingdom,   through his High Lord's
                    grace,
Days everlasting   and endless riches,
As no man knoweth them   here in the world. Never

[1] Lacuna in MS.

86

May he think so widely,   the thane in his mind,
Nor may the heart of a man   hold it and grasp it
To know most verily what good   All-Wielding God
Hath made ready   so that for each man
All standeth open —   for each who loveth Him well
And hath kept his soul   so turned ever
That he will here enter   the light of the Lord."

XXXI

So He taught them with words;   and a wide crowd
Stood 'round God's Bairn   and busily hearkened,
As He told with His words the way   of the world through
            His parables many.
He told how an aethling   once sowed an acre
Of fine corn with his hands,   good grain in the field.
He wanted to gain   the most winsome of growths,
The fairest of fruits.   But his foe did follow him
With treacherous mind;   and with tares he sowed over
            the top,
With the worst of weeds.   And they waxed there both,
The corn and the tares.   So came along
The husbandmen to the house,   and told this to him, to
            their lord,
The thanes to the warden   with honest words.
"Why, thou didst sow fine grain,   master most good,
Unmixed on this acre.   Yet each earl can see
Nought but weeds are waxing.   Well, how can that be?"
There spake again the aethling,   the man to his earls,
To his vassals the warder;   quoth that he could well
            understand
That an unfriendly man   had sown after him,
That his foe had slyly sown weeds: "These fruits he be-
           grudgeth me so,
That for me he hath stamped out this growth."   Then to
           him spoke again
His friends, his followers,   quoth that they would fare
           there,

Go with force   and would uproot the growth,
The weeds with their hands.   Then their lord spake once
                        more unto them:
"I would not that ye weed them,"   quoth he, "since
                        ye cannot avoid it,
Cannot prevent in your passing,   though ye do it un-
                        gladly,
That ye kill young sprouts   and corn aplenty,
Fell them under your feet.   Henceforth let both
Wax together,   till the harvest doth come
And the fruits are ripe   in the fields,
Ready all on the acre.   Then to that acre
Let us fare; with our hands fetch   and gather the fair
                        grain,
The pure corn cleanly together,   keep it stored in my
                        halls,
So that not a speck   can be spoiled. Take ye the weeds
Bind them in bundles   and cast them into bitter fire.
Let the hot flames   fetch them away,
The insatiable blaze."   Then many an earl stood silent,
Many a thane in thought,   pondering what the Glorious
                        Christ,
The Mighty, the Master   of Men, could mean
And proclaim with His parables,   the Most Priceless of
                        Bairns.
Most eagerly they bade   their Master Good
To unlock the lesson,   so that the land-folk about
Might henceforth hear it, His Holy Word.   Their Lord here
                        replied unto them —
Famed, Mighty Christ.   "This is," quoth He, "the Son of
                        Man.
I myself am He Who there soweth;   and these blessed men
Who hearken closely to me   are the fair, clean corn.
They do work my will.   This world is the field,
The broad farmland   of the bairns of mankind;
And it is Satan himself   who soweth after Me
Such loathsome lessons.   Of the land-folk so many,

88

Of the people, so many hath he ruined,   so that they
                    wreak much wrong,
Working *his* will.   Yet they shall wax henceforth,
Those men who are damned,   even as do the good,
Until the Judgment Day   journeyeth on over them —
The end of the world.   Each field then, each acre,
Hath ripened all in the realm.   And the children of men
                    will rightly
Finish their fore-ordained fate.   Earth will explode:
That is the broadest of harvests;   and the Bright,
                    Glorious Lord
Cometh above with the force of His angels;   all folk
                    shall gather,
Who have seen this light;   and shall receive such reward,
Both evil and good.   Then God's angels go forth,
Heaven's holy warders;   and from the host
They shall seek out the sinless men;   bring such men to
                    beauty unending,
To the high light of Heaven;   throwing the others to the
                    grounds of hell,
To the surging fire,   those who were forfeited.
There in bonds shall they   suffer the bitter fire,
The awful pain,   while the others have riches
In the kingdom of Heaven,   surely giving light on high,
Like unto white suns.   Such rewards will they reap,
Those men for their murderous deeds.   Whosoever hath
                    wit in his mind,
Thoughts in his heart,   who would like to hear —
An earl with his ears —   let that indeed be his care
In his innermost heart,   how he will face
God the Richest   on that renowned Day of Reckoning
Of all the words and the works   which he hath done in
                    this world.
That is the most awful   of all things indeed,
The most fearful for the folk-bairns: that they must
                    speak face to face with the Lord —
The men to their Master Good;   there would each man

And all most gladly   be rid of his misdeeds,
His ugly sins. Instead   each one should take care
                                    earlier,
All the land-folk ever,   before they must leave this
                                    light,
That they will have   this eternal honor,
The high kingdom of Heaven   and God's holy grace."

XXXII

So I discovered that He Himself,   the Son of God,
The Best of All Bairns   told boldly in parables
What there might be   in the kingdom of world
Among the races of heroes   like unto the kingdom of
                                    Heaven;
Quoth that that which is little   often waxeth lighter,
So that it riseth on high,   "So doeth the realm of
                                    Heaven.
That is ever more   than any one man
Can envision here in this world.   Also his work is like
                                    unto him:
That a man doth cast   his nets into the sea,
Doth fish in the flood,   and findeth both in his
                                    catch —
Both evil and good —   toweth both to the shore,
Getteth them both onto land,   throweth the good on the
                                    grit,
Letteth the other return   again into the sea,
To the wide waves there.   So doeth All-Wielding God
On the best-known Day   to the bairns of men.
He bringeth the earthlings   together all,
Picketh then the pure ones   for the kingdom of Heaven,
Letteth the damned ones   fare down to the bottom,
To the fire of hell.   Nor doth any hero of men
Know how to counter the pain,   which a person,
A man of the folk, must suffer   in infernal hell.
Likewise can no man   find a like reward,

Either in riches or rejoicing,   as the Right-Wielder
                    granteth,
God Himself doth give   to each man of goodness
Who here keepeth himself so,   so that he may enter the
                    kingdom
Of Heaven and the light   that is long, long lasting."
So with His wiles He did teach them.   And the folk
                    wended hence
From all Galilee-land   to see God's Bairn.
They did so for the wonderment,   whence such words came
                    to Him,
So sagely spoken;   that He could say unto them
The Gospel of God   in such goodly fashion,
Could quote it so cleverly.   "He is of these clans here,"
                    quoth they,
"This man through His kinships.   Here is His mother
                    among us,
A wife 'mid this world-folk.   What, we all know them here.
His kinships are all in our ken;   and all of his clans
                    as well.
He waxed 'mid this world-folk.   Whence cometh such wit,
Whence cometh more might   than hath any other man?"
So the men of the land did scorn Him   and spoke on their
                    silly words,
Despised Him, Who was holy,   and would not hear
The Gospel of God.   Because of their great disbelief
He would not make known   His parables many,
His shining tokens,   for He saw the doubt of their minds,
Their wrath-harboring hearts: that here never were
Men so grim-minded 'mongst the Jews   as were in Galilee-
                    land,
So hard of heart.   Though He was the Holy Christ —
As God's Bairn was He born —   they would never believe
Nor piously receive the gospel.   Now the people began
                    to plot,
The world-men to wonder,   how worst of all
They might torment Mighty Christ.   They hight their men,

Their companions come together;   they would accuse Him
Gladly, the Son of God,   accuse Him of sin
With an evil design;   for there was no longing in them
For the Word, for the wise spell;   but they began to
                  speak 'mongst themselves,
How they might cast Him, the Clever   and Strong, over
                  a cliff,
Over a mountain's wall.   The Wielder's Bairn they would
                  kill,
Loose Him from life.   Along with His folk
He fared happily forth.   There was no fear in His heart,
For He knew full well   that the Jewish folk,
That the children of men   could do Him no harm
Because of His godliness   e'er His time was come,
Do no loathsome deeds.   But with that folk He did go,
Climbed high up a cliff,   till they came to the place
Where they planned to cast Him   from the craggy wall,
Fell Him to earth,   that He would forfeit His life,
That His age be ended.   But the minds of the earls
Up high on that mountain,   the bitter thoughts
Of those Jews did pass, so that not a one   possessed
                  such grimness of mind,
Such wrathful spirit,   that he could recognize Christ,
The Son of the Wielder.   But to no one was He known,
No one could recognize Him.   So could He stand 'mid the
                  crowd,
Walk along 'mongst   the multitude there,
Fare forth through the folk.   He found peace for Himself,
Found protection 'gainst the host,   and went forth through
                  their midst,
Through the folk of the foe.   He fared, since He willed so,
Into a wilderness,   the Son of the Wielder,
The Strongest of Kings: He had the power to choose
Where in this land   He would liefer be,
Where in this world   He would tarry.

XXXIII

On another way went John
With his disciples,   the servant of God.
He taught the land-folk   long-lasting counsel:
Said that they should do good,   forsaking all sin,
All misdeeds and murderous works.   To many he was most
dear,
To good men and kind.   There he sought the king of the
Jews,
The leader of his hosts in his house.   Herod he was
hight
For his elders,   this over-proud man.
His bride did bide with him —   she, who had been his
brother's,
His wife in his wide home,   until he went forth
And changed his abode.   Then came the king,
Took this woman for his wife.   There were children
already,
The bairns of his brother.   *He* began to blame her —
John the Good — said   it was repulsive to God,
To the Wielder Himself,   for any world-man to do so:
To take in his bed   the bride of his brother
And have her as wife.   "If thou would'st hear me,
Would'st believe in my lesson, thou should'st have her
no longer,
But in thy mind should'st avoid her: Thou shalt not
have *such* love,
Shalt not sin so greatly."   Sorrow did enter
The woman's heart at these words.   She feared he would
persuade
The world-king with his speech   and his words of wisdom
To leave, to forsake her.   Many loathsome things she
began
To plan and to plot;   and she hight her squires,
Her earls to take captive   the innocent
And put him in prison,   place him in chains,

Lock him in limb-fetters.   She dared not deprive him
                              of life
Because of the folk,   since all were his friends:
They knew him as good   and as worthy of God,
Held him for a soothsayer,   as so well they could.
There was come the time   for the Jew-king's birthday,
As the wise men of the folk   had reckoned well,
That he had been born   and brought to this light.
It was the custom   that each earl should celebrate,
Each man of the Jews mark it with feasting.   There
                              was a mighty crowd
Of men gathered together   in the guest hall,
Leaders and dukes in the house,   since their lord
Was indeed on the king's throne.   Many Jews did come
Into the great hall there.   Glad-hearted were they,
Blithe in their breasts.   They beheld their ring-giver,
Were really in rapture.   Wine was brought to the room,
Clear wine in the bowls,   and the cup-bearers ran back
                              and forth,
Going with golden cups;   gladness was there,
Loud in the halls.   The lords were drinking;
The herdsman of Jews   bethought him with joy,
Pondered how best he might   please the people.
He hight go forth   that gay, young girl,
His brother's bairn,   as he sat on his bench
Haughty with wine;   to the woman he spoke,
Greeted her before the men-guests   and most eagerly bade
                              her,
That she begin some merriment   here before the guests,
Something fair in the feast-hall.   "Let the folk see
What thou hast learned to make   joyous the many,
Make them blithe on the benches;   if thou doest my
                              bidding,
My word before this world-folk;   then will I verily
                              tell unto thee
Loudly before all these landsmen,   and thus let it be
                              done,

94

That I will give unto thee   all that thou asketh
Before these my ring-friends,   though thou demandest
Half of my realm,   half of my kingdom;
So shall I do,   nor shall any world-men
Turn me with words;   but truly it shall be accomplished."
Then the maid was thereafter   inclined in her mind,
In her heart, to her lord,   so that in the house,
In the guest-hall she began   much gaiety now,
Even as the custom   of the folk did command,
The way of the people.   The maid did play,
Most merrily romped through the house.   The minds of the
                              many,
Their hearts were happy.   When the maiden had served
The folk-king there   for his thanks then,
And had served, too, his earlships all,   as many as were
Of good men present,   she would fain claim her gift —
The maid in front of the multitude.   To her mother she
                              went
To speak and asked her forthwith —   for she was anxious
                        to know —
What she should bid him,   bid the bastion's warden give
                        unto her.
Of her own mind her mother did tell her,   hight that
                        before the men
She should ask for naught else   except that he give her
There in the hall   John's holy head
Bereft of its body.   For the folk it was baleful,
For the men in their minds,   when they heard the maid
                        speaking thus,
For the king it was, also;   but he could not break it,
                        his pledge,
Turn his word away.   Therefore he bade the bearers of
                        weapons
To go from the guest hall,   take the good man
And relieve him of life.   Not long thereafter they brought
The holy man's head   up to the hall, gave it the girl,
To the maid before the many.   To her mother she took it.

And that was the end-day   of the wisest of all men,
Who ever came to this world   as a child born of woman,
Of a wife from an earl —   excepting ever that One,
Whom the Maid did bear,   she who had known no man
Anywhere in this world;   but the All-Wielder so destined it
From the fields of Heaven   by the Holy Ghost —
The Mighty God had so marked it.   Never was man like
                         unto him,
Neither before nor after.   Now the earls turned to him,
The men around John,   his followers many,
His beloved disciples.   In the sand they buried
His beloved body.   But well did they know
He could claim God's light,   along with his Lord,
Heavenly glory   in that home on high —
He, who was blessed indeed.

XXXIV

          So his disciples fared thence,
John's followers went,   most woeful of spirit
But holy of mind.   The death of their master
Filled them with sorrow.   They repaired then to seek
The Son of the Wielder   away in the wilderness,
Christ the Almighty,   and made known unto Him
The good man's demise: how the master of Jews
Did heave off the head   of the holiest of men
With the sword's edge.   The Son of the Lord had no wish
To speak of His own pain;   for He knew that this soul
Was held in all holiness   against the haters,
In peace 'gainst the foe.   Thus He grew famous
Across the country,   He, the best of those teaching
In the wilderness there;   world-men did gather;
To the folk He did come,   for they had great longing
For the wisom of words;   and He had long wanted,
The Son of the Lord,   to lead such a gathering
Of the land-folk   to the light of the Lord,
To turn the folk to His will.   The Wielder did teach,

96

The Mighty Lord taught all the long day   so many of
                              mankind,
Folk from all over   and from foreign lands, until in the
                              evening
The sun did sink to its seat.   Then His disciples twelve
Did go to God's Bairn   and told their Good Lord
In what dire need the men did there dwell;   quoth that
                    they did need His help,
The world-folk in the wilderness there;   "Not well can
                    they hold themselves upright,
The heroes, for the pangs of their hunger;   now, Lord Good
                    and Most High,
Let them go to find lodgings.   Nearby lie towns
Filled with folk aplenty;   there they will find meat
                              to buy,
The world-folk there in those bailiwicks."   Thereupon
                    Wielding Christ spoke again,
The Lord of the Land-folk,   quoth that there was little
                              need,
"That they forsake   My fair teachings
Because of their poverty.   Give these people enough.
Let them come here gladly!"   His words had he ready,
The wise man named Philip;   quoth that there were so
                              many,
Such a multitude of mankind,   "Though we might have
                              meat
Ready to give them,   were we able to buy it
And for that sold together   two hundred pieces of silver,
Still would I doubt   that each would have some.
So little were that for these land-folk."   Then again
                    the Land-Warder spoke
And asked them,   anxious for knowledge,
The Master of Men,   how much of meat,
Of food they had gathered.   Then again with his words
Andrew did speak before the earls   to the All-Wielder
                              Himself,
And said now to Him   that they had naught for the journey,

97

"Naught but five breads of barley   among the followers,
                    and fishes twain:
How can that serve such a many?"   Mighty Christ spake
                    again,
The Good Son of God,   and hight they divide into groups,
The crowd, into sections;   and hight they should sit,
All the lords, on the ground;   the hordes of the land-folk
                    should lie
On the green grass;   and to His followers goodly he spoke,
The Best of All Bairns;   hight them go bring the bread
And fetch forth the fish.   The folk bided still —
The great crowd was sitting.   Through His strength and
                    His power
The Lord of Mankind at this moment   did bless the meat,
The Holy Heaven-King,   and with His hands He did break it,
And to His disciples He gave it,   hight that they should
                    take it and divide it
Among the multitude there.   Their Master's word they ac-
                    complished.
To each man gladly   they carried His gift,
The holy help.   It waxed in their hands,
The meat for each man: for the multitude
There came a life full of joy;   the landsmen all,
The folk had their fill —   as many as had fared there
                    together
From all the wide ways.   Then Wielding Christ
Hight His disciples go,   and hight them watch well,
That the leavings left there   would not be lost,
Commanded them gather   the many of mankind
When they had had their fill.   There was left of the
                    food,
Of the bread so much,   that they gathered baskets —
Twelve of them filled.   That was a great token,
A great deed of God,   since one counted together,
Without wife or child,   of world-folk there,
Fully five thousand.   The folk understood,
The men in their minds,   that it was a Lord Most Mighty

Whom they did have.   They did laud the Heaven-King,
The people did praise Him;   said that no wiser prophet
Would ever fare in this light   or that from God
He would have greater might   in this mid-world here,
A more honest heart.   All of them did say
That He was worthy   of holding all wealth,
That indeed He should own   all the realms of earth,
The wide throne of world,   "since He hath such wit,
Such great power from God!"   The people all thought it
                    meet
That they raise Him   to the highest of hights,
Choose Him their King: to Christ this was worthy of
                    naught,
Since He Himself had worked   this world-realm all through
                    his power alone,
Had made earth and the high heaven,   and had held them since,
Both the land and the landsmen —   but the loathsome foe
Believed naught of that: that all stood 'neath His rule —
The power over kingdoms   and over empires, too,
The judgment of man.   Still through the speech of these
                    men
He cared not to have it, His rule —   He, Holy Lord —
Have the name of World-King.   Therefore He began no further
                    word-strife
With these people there;   but He went where He willed
Up on a mountain;   God's Mighty Bairn fled
The insolent talk,   and He told His disciples
To sail over a sea;   and He Himself said
Where they should go   to greet Him again.

                    XXXV

The people parted   and spread through all lands,
A great folk scattered,   for their Lord had gone
Up on the mountain,   the Mightiest of Bairns,
Wielding as was His will.   On the water's shore
Gathered the disciples of Christ,   whom He Himself had
                    chosen,

The twelve for their goodly faith;   nor felt they doubt;
But in God's service   they would gladly go
Over the sea.   They let the high-horned ship
Cut through the strong stream,   the clear wave and the
                                            water sheer;
The light of the day, the sun strode to rest.   Night
                                            surrounded
The seafarers with mist;   the earls strove on,
Forward in the flood.   Now the fourth hour
Of night was come.   All-Saving Christ
Warded the wave-farers: the wind grew great,
The sea 'gainst the stem;   with trouble they steered it,
The ship through the wind.   The warriors grew fearful of
                                            mind,
Their hearts filled with care.   The lake-farers indeed
Never believed   that they would ever reach land
Because of the battle of weather.   There they beheld
                                            Christ,
The Wielder, walking   over the waves on the sea,
Faring on foot.   Into the flood he could
Not sink, not sink into the sea;   for the power of Him
                                            Himself
Held Him on high.   Their hearts became fearful,
The minds of the men.   They feared the mighty Fiend
Had done this to deceive Him.   Then their Dear Lord did
                                            speak unto them,
The Holy Heaven-King;   and said that *He* was their Lord,
Splendid and Mighty.   "Now in your minds
Shall ye all take courage;   nor be ye frightened of
                                            spirit.
But behave ye boldly: for I am God's Bairn,
The Son of Himself,   and against the sea I shall help
                                            you,
Against these flood-streams."   Then a man did answer
From upon the ship,   a sage most worthy,
Peter the good: that no longer   he wished to endure the
                                            pain,

The woe of the water,   "If Thou beest the Wielder,
Master Most Good,   as I think in my mind,
Bid me come unto Thee   across the flood of the sea,
Dry over the deep water —   if Thou art indeed my Lord,
The Master of Many."   Then Mighty Christ
Hight him come unto Him.   He was soon ready,
Stepped on the stem;   and striding, he went
Forth to the Lord;   the flood held him upright,
The man through God's might,   until in his mind he began
To dread the deep water,   when he saw it driven —
The wave — by the wind: The flood wound around him,
The billows about him.   But even as in his mind he did
                    doubt,
So the water grew weak beneath him.   And into the wave,
Into the sea-stream he sank;   and straightway he called
To the Bairn of God   and eagerly bade Him,
That He save him there,   since he, His thane, was
In distress and in need.   Then the Lord of the Nations
Embraced him with His hands and His arms,   and straight-
                    way did ask him,
Why he was doubtful.   "Why, thou should'st trust well
And know most verily   that the might of the water,
Of the sea itself   could not hinder thy steps,
That of the lake-flood thy feet   for as long as thou
                    believest in Me,
In thy heart hath a faith steadfast.   Now I shall help thee,
In thy need shall save thee."   The Almighty so took him,
The Holy Man by the hand: here again the clear water
Became firm under foot,   and they fared together
Both step in step,   until they came aboard ship,
Stepped from the stream.   And at the stem
Sat the Best of All Bairns.   Then the broad water,
The stream became stilled;   and they came to the shore,
The landfarers indeed   did come to the land
Through the battle of waters;   and said thanks to the
                    Wielder,
Gave praise to their Dear Lord   in deed and in word.

They fell to His feet   and did speak full many
Words of wisdom;   quoth that they right well knew
That He Himself   was verily the Son of the Lord
Here in the world   and wielded power
Over the middle earth;   and all men He could help,
Whosoever they were,   as He had done on the flood
'Gainst the battle of waters.

XXXVI

Then All-Wielding Christ
Turned His steps from the sea: The Son of the Lord,
God's only Child.   Heathens did come to Him,
Foreign folk fared to Him there.   For from afar
They had heard of His good works: that so many true words
He did speak; for He longed greatly   to further such
                    folk,
So that straightway   they would serve God gladly,
Becoming true vassals   of the King of Heaven,
The many of mankind.   So He made His way across Judea,
Sought out the city of Sidon;   His disciples He had with
                    Him,
Christ's followers good.   There a woman came toward Him
From another tribe: of aethling birth was she,
From the kith of Canaan-land;   she bade the Lord Christ
                    so strong,
The Holy One, to grant her His help: quoth that great
                    trouble had come to her,
Sorrow for the sake of her daughter;   said she was en-
                    snared by sickness,
Deceived by treacherous devils.   "Now is her death at
                    hand.
The wrathful wights have robbed her of wit.   Now I beg
                Thee, my All-Wielding Ruler,
Thou Son of David himself,   from such sickness release
                    her,
That Thou mayest mercifully   protect this poor maid

From the grievous devils." But All-Wielding Christ gave
Her no answer. Therefore she went after Him,
Followed Him boldly, till she came to His feet,
And weeping did speak unto Him. The disciples of Christ
Bade the Master that He be mild in His heart
To the woman. Then had ready His word
The Son of the Lord, and unto His disciples He spoke:
"First shall I be of use to the folkships here,
To the people of Israel, so that a pious spirit
They shall have for their Lord. For they are in need of
  help:
The land-folk are lost; they have left and forsaken
The word of the Wielder; with doubts are they troubled —
  these people —
Harboring treacherous hearts. Nor is the host of Israel
Willing to hear their Lord; but they are unbelieving,
The men in their Master. Then to the rest of mankind
Help shall come later." Lo, most zealously then
The woman begged with her words, that All-Wielding
  Christ
Become mildly inclined, that she might henceforth enjoy
Her child, having her hale. Then the Lord spoke to her,
The Magnificent and Mighty. "No man," quoth He, "hath
  the right,
No person ever, to do good or give alms in such manner,
That his own bairns will be bereft of their bread,
Deprived 'gainst their will, so that they suffer great
  pain,
Grim, hateful hunger; and feedeth his hound-dogs with
  their food."
"True it is, Wielder," quoth she, "what Thou speakest
  indeed with Thy words,
Most truly dost say. Why, oft 'neath the tables
In the halls of the lords, the puppies hop hither
And yon for the crumbs, full many of which fall
From the board of their master." The Peace-Bairn
  of God heard

The will of the woman,   and with words He did speak:
"Well that thou, wife,   hast goodness of will.
Great is thy faith   in the power of God,
In the Lord of the Land-folk.   Lo, all will be done
For the life of thy bairn,   even as thou hast bidden of
                Me!"
And straightway was she healed,   as the Holy Lord had
                said
With words of truth;   and the wife was happy
That henceforth she would be blessed   with joy in her
                bairn.
Christ the Healer   had helped her indeed,
Had snatched her away   from the strength of the Fiend,
Guarded her against the loathsome wight.   The Wielder
                went forth.
The Best of All Bairns   sought Him another borough,
Which was so thick   with the throngs of the Jews,
Settled with south-dwellers.   There, I discovered,
He greeted His followers   whom in His goodness he had
                chosen,
Disciples who gladly stayed for His wise speech.   "I
                shall ask of you all,
With My words," quoth He, "My followers: What say the
                Jews,
That notorious folk,   who I am among men?"
Happily His friends   gave answer to Him,
His disciples: "The Jewish folk," they said,
"The earls are not of one mind.   Some say Thou art Elias,
The soothsayer wise,   who was here long ago,
A good earl among these folk;   some say Thou art John,
Our Dear Lord's herald,   who once did dip
The world-folk in water.   But with words they all say,
That Thou art some sort of noble,   some aethling man,
Some soothsayer or prophet,   who hath taught the people
Once before with his words.   And once again Thou art come
                to this light
To teach the kith of mankind."   Wielding Christ spake
                again:

"What quoth ye that I be?"   quoth He, "My followers,
My landsmen beloved?"   Then not late with his words was he,
Simon Peter;   but straightway he spoke —
One for them all —   of good spirit was he:
Daring in thought,   he was dear to the Lord.

XXXVII

"Thou art truly   the All-Wielder's Son,
The Living God,   who created the light,
Christ, King Eternal: so willingly do we quoth,
We Thy disciples,   that Thou art God Himself,
The Best of All Healers."   Then his Lord spoke to him,
"So blessed art thou, Simon," quoth He,   "Son of Jonas,
            thou thyself couldst not have
Marked such thoughts in thy mind;   nor could any man's
                        tongue
Show thee with words.   But the Wielder Himself did this
                        for thee,
The Father of All Folk-Bairns,   that thou spakest so
                        forthright,
So deep of thy Liege.   Dear shall be thy reward,
Limpid and pure thy belief in thy Lord: like unto a
                        stone is thy spirit.
So strong art thou like unto a rock;   and the children
                    of men shall call thee
Saint Peter; and on this stone   men shall build My great
                        hall,
God's holy house.   There shall His family, His household
All gather, blessed, together,   and against thy strength,
Thy power, the portals of hell cannot stand.   To thee I
                    present it,
The key to Heaven's kingdom,   so that o'er the Christian
                        folk
Thou shalt after Me have the most might;   the spirits
                        of men
Shall all come to thee;   for thou shalt claim great
                        power

O'er the bairns of mankind.   Whomsoever thou would'st
bind
Here on this earth: for him both is done,
For him the kingdom of heaven is locked   and for him
hell lieth open,
The burning fire;   and whomsoever thou would'st again
unbind,
Whose hands unfetter: for him is Heaven's kingdom
Unlocked, the greatest of lights,   and life everlasting,
God's fair, green meadows.   With such gifts I would
Reward thee thy faith.   Still I would not that ye pro-
claim now to the folk,
To the multitude yet,   that I be the Mighty Christ,
The Own Bairn of God.   For the Jews shall still bind Me,
In guiltiness tie Me   and torture Me most terribly,
Do Me great wrongs   here in Jerusalem,
With spear-point attacking,   with the sharp edge against
Me,
Relieve Me of life.   Through the power of the Lord here
in this light
I shall arise though from death   on the third day."
Then in sorrow was he,   Simon Peter, the best of all
thanes;
Most grieved he of mind.   And to the Master he spoke,
The warrior in whispers.   "That is not the will of the
Wielder,
Of Mighty God," quoth he.   "It cannot be that Thou
should'st endure
Such pain 'mid this people.   There is plainly no need,
O Holy Master!"   Then Christ Mighty and Marvelous,
The Lord, did reply —   he was dear to His heart —
"Why," quoth He,   "thou art now opposed to My will,
Thou best of My thanes?   Thou knowest this folk,
Hast ken of the customs of men.   But God's might, which
I must accomplish,
That wittest thou not.   With words of truth
I can tell thee much: that here 'mid the people stand

Disciples of Mine   who shall not die,
Not begin the trip hence,   before they shall see Heaven's
                                light,
The kingdom of God."   From His disciples He chose
Soon after that   Simon Peter,
Jacob and John,   those good men twain,
Both of the brothers.   And He betook Himself then upon
                                a mountain
With His disciples aside from the others —   God's Bairn
                                so blessed
With His thanes three;   Lord of this Folk,
Wielder of World,   He would show unto them
Wonders a-many, such tokens,   so that they should trust
                                and believe
That He Himself   was the Son of the Lord,
The Holy Heaven-King.   At a high wall
They climbed stone and cliff,   till they came to a
                                place,
These men, close to the clouds,   which All-Wielding
                                Christ,
The Strongest of Kings,   had Himself chosen,
That He would reveal   most verily His godliness
To His disciples,   His divinity —
A bright, shining picture.

XXXVIII

When He bent low in prayer,
Lo, there upon the mountain   His whole appearance,
His garb became changed.   His cheeks became light,
Shone like the bright, shimmering sun: so shone God's
                                Bairn.
Light was His body,   and long rays shone
Radiant around the All-Wielder's Bairn,   His raiment
                                so white
To the sight as is snow.   Then a marvel was shown
Up there on the mountain: Elias and Moses

Did come there to Christ   to exchange words with Him,
The Strongest of Kings.   There was winsome conversing,
Good words among men;   where the Son of God
Would fain have talk   with those famous men.
So blithe it was, up there on the mountain.   And the light
                    shone bright,
And it was like unto that goodly garden,   that meadow green,
Like unto Paradise itself.   And Peter there spoke,
Hero hardy of spirit   and to His Lord he did speak,
Greeted the Son of God,   "Good it is to be here,
If Thou hast so chosen,   O Christ All-Wielding,
That men on these hights   build Thee a house,
Make it most splendid;   and for Moses a second;
And a third for Elias.   This is the home of joy,
The most winsome possession."   Just as he spoke these
                    words,
The air clove in twain: from the clouds light shone
                    clear,
A glistening glow.   And the good men
Were wrapped in a radiance.   Then from the clouds rolled
God's holy voice.   And to the heroes there
He Himself said   that this was His Son,
The Most Beloved of the Living: "I like Him well,
To My heart He is dear.   Ye shall hear Him,
Following Him gladly."   Then the followers of Christ,
Those men, could not withstand   the cloud's clear light,
The word of God   and its might, which is great.
But they fell forward,   and they feared indeed
They would lose their lives.   Then the Land-Warden did go
                    to them;
And with His hand He touched them,   the Best of Healers,
Hight they should feel no dread: "No harm shall
                    come to you here
From these blessed sights   which ye have now seen,
These marvelous things."   Then the men's spirits
In their hearts were healed,   and healed were their minds;
In their breasts there was comfort: for they saw God's
                    Bairn

Standing alone.   The other, though,
Heaven's light, was again hidden.   Then the Holy Christ
Went Him down from the mountain,   and He did then bid
His followers that they tell not   unto the Jewish folk
Of the sight they had seen.   "Until I Myself here
In splendor shall   stand up from My death,
Arise from My rest.   Then may ye relate it,
Spread it over the mid-earth   and its many peoples,
Wide o'er this world.

XXXIX

Then Wielding Christ
Went again to Galilee-land.   Great Christ sought His
landsmen,
The home of His kin.   With bright, clear pictures
He spoke much unto them.   And the Son of God
Concealed not sorrowful tidings   from His blessed dis-
ciples,
But openly He said   all things to them,
His followers good,   how the Jewish folk
Would torture Him all terribly.   Then troubled were they,
The wise men, greatly,   and grieved at heart,
Saddened of spirit,   when they heard their Lord,
The Son of the Wielder,   telling with words
What He would endure   here midst the earth-folk,
Willingly all among the people of world.   Then All-Wield-
ing Christ,
The Man, went from Galilee   and sought a city of Jews.
They came to Capernaum.   There He found a king's thane,
Proud 'mid the people; quoth   that he was the trusted
courier
Of the noble emperor;   he greeted thereafter
Simon Peter; and said   he had been sent here
That he remind   each man and every
Of his head-tax   which he must pay as a tithe
Here to the court: "Nor can any man hesitate,

But he payeth unto him   his choicest treasure.
Only your Master alone   hath omitted His tithe,
Hath neglected it.   Nor will my lord like this,
When they inform him of this,   the aethling emperor."
Then Simon Peter went straightway.   He so wanted
To tell this unto His Master.   But in His mind
Holy Christ already knew;   for from Him naught could be
                              hidden,
Not even a word;   but He well knew indeed
The mind of each man;   but he admonished His thane,
Simon Peter of fame,   that into the sea
He should cast his hook.   "Whatsoever thou dost catch,
What fish at the first," quoth He,   "from the flood
                              thou must draw it,
Wedge open its jaws: from under its chin mayest thou
                              take
Golden guilders,   with which thou shalt give
The man enough of the tax   which he seeketh from us, from
                              Me and from thee."
He needed bid him   thereafter no more,
Give him no other words: but the Good Fisher did go,
Simon Peter;   into the sea he did cast
His angle, his hook in the wave;   and verily then
He drew a fish   from the flood. Its jaws
He tore open with his two hands.   And from under its
                              chin took
The golden guilders.   And all he so did as God's Son
Had told him with words.   So was the strength of the
                              Wielder,
His might made manifest,   how each man and all
Should most willingly pay   to his world-lord here
The taxes and tolls   determined against him,
And do so gladly;   nor should any forget this,
Neglect or deny in his mind;   but mild in his heart,
He should serve him humbly.   So should he work
The will of God   and still gain the grace
Of his worldy master.

XL

So Holy Christ did teach
His disciples good: "If against you," quoth He, "any man
Do act in sin,   then take ye this man aside,
This warrior, with whispers,   and speak ye wise counsel
And teach him with words.   Should he not be worthy
To hear your teachings,   then fetch ye hither
Other men and good;   and with his grim works reproach him,
Say them forth most soothly.   If then his sins
His evil deeds do not grieve him,   so make ye them open
              to others,
Most revealed to the multitude,   and let many men
Know his wrongs. Then easily   he will repent his works,
In his heart indeed rue them,   when he heareth that so
              many folk,
Bairns of mankind have watched them   and warded off
              with their words
The works of his evil.   If even then he will not change,
But scorneth such a many,   then let this man fare forth,
Believe him a heathen,   and let him be loathsome unto
              you in your hearts.
In your minds avoid him,   unless God the Mild,
The High King of Heaven,   grant help unto him,
The Father of All Folk-Bairns."   Peter then asked,
The best of all thanes   then questioned the Lord,
"How often shall I absolve   from sin this man
Who hath done loathsome work   against me, Beloved Lord?
How many times shall I   take from him all his blame
For his wicked works,   before rewarding the wrongs
By wreaking vengeance?"   Then spoke again the Warden
              of the Land.
The Son of God did give answer   unto His goodly thane:
"I shall never say unto thee: seven,   as thou thyself
              hast spoken,
Hast made known with thy mouth.   I add more thereto:
Seven times seventy!   So shalt thou absolve each one

From evil, from sin.   So I would give unto thee
Teachings, a word most true.   Since to thee I have lent
the power,
That thou beest the highest one   of my household
To many of mankind;   so shalt thou be mild unto them,
Merciful unto the multitude."   Then a young man
Came to the Teacher,   and Jesus Christ he did question:
"Master Most Good," quoth he,   "What must I do,
So that I may reach   the realms of Heaven?"
All goodly riches   had he gained indeed,
Many a treasure, too,   though mildness of heart
He bore in his breast.   Then spake God's Bairn unto him;
"Why speakest thou of a Good One?   There is no man
But that One Single One,   who shaped this All —
This world in its winsomeness.   If 'tis thy will,
Then shalt thou hold   to the holy teachings,
Those which the Old Law   command thee follow:
That thou shalt not slay;   nor swear falsely,
Neither commit adultery;   nor bear thou false witness
Nor steal nor cause strife;   nor be thou too stubborn
of mind,
Nor hating nor hateful;   commit thou no robbery.
Forsake thou all envy;   to thine elders show kindness,
To thy father and mother.   Be thou fair to thy friends,
To thy nearest be gracious.   Then wilt thou be granted
joy
In the kingdom of Heaven,   if thou wilt keep this
And follow God's teachings."   Again the young man did
speak:
"All things have I done,"   quoth he, "as thou now dost
teach
And tellest with words;   that I have no whit left undone
Since the days of my childhood."   Then Christ did begin
To turn His eyes onto him.   "One thing," He told him,
"Is still lacking in thy works.   If thou hast the will,
That thou would'st serve   thy Lord most perfectly still,
Then shalt thou take   thy hoard and thy treasure;

Thou shalt rid thyself   of thy riches all,
Order thy precious jewels   to be portioned out
And shared with the poor.   Then shalt thou have
A hoard in Heaven.   Come thou then as healed unto Me
And follow My path.   Then shalt thou have peace ever
                after."
Then the words of the Christ   caused great worry and care
To the child-young man.   His mind was sore,
About his heart his spirit.   For he had great wealth,
Had won great treasure;   he again turned away.
In his breast he felt   burdened indeed,
In his heart most heavy.   Then Christ looked after him,
The All-Wielder,   since He so willed,
And said to His disciples, who were there,   that it was
                even so hard
For a rich man to reach   the realms of Heaven:
"More easily may an elephant,   though it be unseemly
                great,
Go through a needle's eye,   be that eye so narrow —
Slip through more softly,   than this soul into Heaven,
The soul of this wealthy man,   who hath turned his will
                to world-things entirely,
The thoughts of his mind,   and mindeth not the great
                might of God."

XLI

Him answered then   an aethling most excellent and honored,
Simon Peter;   and speaking, he bade
His Blessed Lord: "What reward shall we look for,
What goods to repay us —   we, who have forsaken
Our lands and our heritage   for love of Thy following,
Our farmyards and families,   and chosen Thee for our Lord,
Following Thy footsteps?   What good will there be for us,
What long-lasting reward?"   The Lord of the Land-folk
Himself said unto them: "When I shall come to sit,"
              quoth He

"In My might and My power   on that most Renowned Day,
When I shall deal out   the dooms to the people of earth,
Then may ye sit with your Master,   may wield His affairs —
Ye may judge Israel's   aethling folk
By its deeds: so honored   will ye be up there.
For I verily say unto you: whosoever acteth on this earth,
So that for My love   he leaveth the dear home of his kin,
He shall receive   a tenfold reward, if he acteth
Loyally, with pureness of heart.   Above shall he have
                                        Heaven's light.
Eternal life will lie open."   Therefore the Lord,
The Best of all Bairns,   began to speak pictures,
Told how a man of great fortune   in former days
Lived 'mongst the land-folk: "He had laid aside wealth,
Gathered great treasures unto him;   and ever with gold
He was decked and with silken stuff   and with the sheen
Of fine jewels; and so many goods   he had stored away
In his buildings;   and at banquet
He sat every day.   There was splendid carousing
And joy on his benches.   There was a beggar-man also:
Lame of limb was he   and Lazarus hight;
And every day he did lie   in front of the door,
Where he knew the rich man   received food in the guest-
                                        hall
And sat at his banquet;   and outside bided
The poor man; nor was he   ever permitted within,
Nor could he bring it about   by his begging that bread
Be brought out to him,   such bread as had fallen from
                                        the dish
Down beneath their feet.   Not a thing did he gain
From the high man who ruled over the house;   but only the
                                        hounds of that man
Came and licked on his wounds,   as he lay there
And endured his hunger.   Not one whit of help
Came from the man of fortune.   Then I found out that fate
Admonished the poor man   most mightily
Of his end-days: that he should renounce

His life and the tumult of men.   The Lord's angels
Did receive his spirit   and so led him from there,
So that the poor man's soul   did sit in the lap
Of Abraham. Ever henceforth   he could now dwell
In all winsomeness.   Then Weird came also,
That fateful hour,   to the man of fortune,
So that he should forsake this light;   the loathsome
                    wights
Lowered his soul, sank it   deep into swarthy hell,
In the furnace below   to the will of the Fiend,
Grubbed him deep into the Grim One's home.   There he
                    could gaze on
The good man, see Abraham,   where he dwelt above
In a life of joy;   and Lazarus sat
Blithe in his bosom;   received bright reward
For his poverty and wretchedness all.   And the rich man
                    there
Lay hot in hell,   and he did cry up from there:
"Father Abraham," quoth he,   "It is fearfully needful for
                    me,
That thou becomest mild   to me in thy mind,
Merciful unto me in this flame.   Send Lazarus unto me,
That he fetch cold water   for me in this furnace.
Hotly I burn alive in this hell   and I am in need of thy
                    help,
That he slake my tongue   with his little finger.
My tongue hath its token now: woeful torture for my
                    evil counsel,
For my sinful speech.   Now is come to me such reward!"
Abraham answered unto him —   he was the ancient father —
"Ponder in thy heart," quoth he,   "what thou hast had
Of wealth in the world.   Why, thou hast wasted thy rap-
                    ture all,
Thy goods in the gardens,   and what was to be given
Hence unto thee.   Lazarus here
Endured wrong in the light;   had plenteous grief
And pain in the world.   For this he shall now have wealth,

Living in happiness.   But thou shalt suffer hot flames,
The burning fire.   Nor may any betterment
Come hither to hell.   So hath Holy God
Made it fast with hands and with arms;   nor may any one
                    fare,
Any thane through the darkness —   it is here too thick
                    under us."
Then the earl spake again   to Abraham:
From that hot hell   did he beg for help,
That he do send   Lazarus himself
Down to the tumult of men,   "so that he may tell
Unto those brethren mine   how I here burn
And suffer great pain.   Among the people,
The folk, there are five: I am in great fear
That they shall also become sinful   and shall suffer such
                    pangs
In this great fire."   Then again spoke unto him
Old Father Abraham,   quoth that they ever had had —
The folk — the old law   there in their land,
The commandments of Moses,   and from many a prophet
Their words also.   "If they are willing
To hold and to keep them,   then need they never enter
                    into hell,
To sear in that fire.   If they so fulfill that
Which those do bid them   who read in the books
To teach mankind.   But if they are unwilling to accom-
                    plish that,
They will also not listen to Him,   who riseth from here,
A Man from death.   In their minds let them
Choose for themselves   which seemeth sweeter
To win so long   as they are still in this world,
So that in the hereafter   they have evil or good!"

XLI

So did He teach the land-folk all   with His words of
                    light,

The Best of All Bairns;   and with bright pictures
A-many, the Mighty Lord   did speak to mankind:
Quoth that a blessed man   had begun to gather
Men in the morning,   promised them money —
He, the first of his family —   a very fine reward:
Said that unto each   and to all he would give
A coin of pure silver.   So came together
Many men in the winegarden —   and he commanded their work —
Gathered early at morn.   Then also others did come in
                    the forenoon,
And some came at the midday —   the men to the work;
Some came then at nones,   that was a late time
Of the summer-long day.   Some even later did come:
At the eleventh hour it was.   And the evening arrived
And the sun went to rest.   Then he himself bade
His overseers all,   this lord of earls,
That they give unto each man   his money and pay,
To each workman his rightful reward;   hight that they
                    were to give first,
To those who had been last,   the land-folk in coming,
The workers to work;   and with his words he commanded them
To give unto those men   their mite last of all:
To those who had come there first willingly   to the work.
                    They weened greatly
That they should receive   a larger reward,
More pay for their work;   but to all the people
Was equally given.   Then were they angered,
Were all in a fury,   those who came first to that place.
"In the morning we came here,"   quoth they, "and toiled
                    much of the day
In hard work, in labor   during the unmeasured heat,
In the shining sun.   Now thou givest unto us no more of
                    silver
Than thou dost to the others,   who were here only a while
Doing their work."   Then had ready his word
The head of the household;   quoth that he had not pro-
                    mised them

More pay for their work. "What,"   quoth he, "I wield
                    here the power
To give to each man and all   an equal reward,
Equal pay for his work."   Thus All-Wielding Christ
Meant, however, a mightier thing,   when He spoke to the
                    men,
Gave the folk such a word   about the wine-garden,
How the workers did come   in an unlike way,
The men to their work.   So shall the bairns of this
                    world,
The children of mankind,   do in that clear, marvelous
                    light,
Men on God's meadow;   some may begin to prepare themselves
Already in childhood.   Such a spirit is chosen,
His will is good, and he   avoideth the ways of the world,
Leaveth behind him his lusts.   He will never let it, his
                    body,
Entice him to evil;   but eagerly he learneth
Wisdom and the law of God,   and leaveth behind
The will of the devil, the dire foe: so doeth he ever in
                    this world!
He is so in this light,   until there cometh of life,
Of all age the evening;   and he fareth thence and up on
                    his way.
There his work all   will be rewarded,
Repaid with good   in the realm of God.
Thereby was meant those workmen   who in the morning
Early began with their work,   who until evening
Did so continue their tasks.   Some also came to the work
At the midmorn,   having squandered the morning
And spoiled their day's duties.   So do many dullards,
Frivolous folk.   For much folly have they done,
Varied deeds in their youth.   Yea, they have learned
                    wrong,
Have learned scornful speech   and such words of evil,
Until their childhood   passeth away.
And after their young years   God's grace doth admonish
                    them

Blithe in their breasts.   They turn to the better,
Both in words and in works,   and lead well their lives
To their very ends.   And rewards come to them
For all their good works   in the kingdom of God.
Some men, however,   forsake their sin
Not until mid-life, their dire misdeeds,   turning their
                              minds
To blessed things; and they begin   good works through the
                         power of God
And repent their wrong talk   and rue their bitter deeds
Well in their hearts;   there cometh to them help from God,
So that they believe   as long as life keepeth within
                              them:
With that they fare forth   and receive their reward,
A goodly prize from Lord God;   nor are there gifts any
                         better.
Some begin still later,   when they have become old already
And their age grows to its end;   then their evil works be-
                         gin to be
Loathsome to them in this light;   and the learning of God
Admonishes them in their minds   and their hearts become
                         milder.
They do good deeds to the end   of their days and reap
                         their reward,
The high kingdom of Heaven,   when they repair from here,
Receive their rewards,   as those men did reap theirs
Who came to the work   in the vineyards there
At the none of the day,   at the ninth hour indeed.
Yet some grow so ancient   and still have not atoned for
                         their sins,
But increase them with every evil,   until their evening
                         doth come unto them,
And their world and its winsomeness passeth away;   then
                    they begin to dread their reward;
Their sins make them sorrowful quite in their hearts.   They
                    ponder sadly that they themselves
Have done wrongs as long as they possessed   their
                    power, nor can they repent,

Atone for their deeds by other good deeds   done so well —
                    but every day
They beat their breasts with their hands   and they weep
                    bitter tears,
Crying out loud their lament,   begging their Holy Lord,
The Mighty God that He grow mild;   nor doth He permit
                    their minds to despair —
So merciful is He, who wieldeth His might over all.   The
                    longing of no man on earth
Doth He want to reject;   but the Wielder Himself doth
                    grant unto him
The holy kingdom of Heaven.   Help is come to him later.
All shall receive their reward,   though they are not come
All at one time, the kith of mankind.   Still the Lord,
                    mighty and wise,
Giveth pay to all people,   whosoever receiveth His belief:
One kingdom of Heaven: He granteth to all the kith of this
                    earth
A reward, to all men.   Mighty Christ did mean that,
The Best of All Bairns,   when He spoke His parables
Of how the workers   came to the wine-gardens,
The men, all differently.   Yet each did receive
Full pay from his liege.   Likewise shall the children of
                    earth
Receive their reward   from Righteous God Himself,
Most lovely pay,   though some come so late.

                    XLIII

Then He hight them,   His disciples,
His followers twelve come closer: they were the truest of
                    men
On this earth unto Him.   And the Mighty One did explain
Unto them one more time   what troubles there were
Standing before them.   "No doubt can there be," quoth He.
Quoth they should go to Jerusalem   to the folk of the Jews.
"There shall all things be accomplished   amid the people

And be brought to pass, even as   in earlier times
Wise men did speak   with their words about Me.
Among the strong folk   there they shall sell Me,
The men to the host.   Then shall my hands be held bound,
My arms and fingers be fettered;   full much shall I suffer,
Scorn shall I hear,   and hurtful speech,
Mockery much   and many a threat.
They will torture Me wounded   with the edge of their
weapons,
Rob me of life. But through the might   and the strength
of the Lord,
I shall arise again on the third day   from death to this
light.
I have not come, however,   to the people here,
So that the children of men   have labor for Me,
That the landsmen should serve Me,   nor shall I so ask them,
Make such demands of the kith   of mankind; but I shall be
of use
Unto them, serving them meekly.   And for all those men
I shall give My soul.   And I Myself
Will release them with My life —   those who bide here so
long —
The many of mankind   awaiting My help."
Then He fared foreward.   For He had firmness of spirit
Blithe in His breast —   the Bairn of the Lord.
He would seek in Jerusalem   the folk of the Jews:
That was His will.   Well did He know
The hate-raging hearts of the people   and the hard strife
And their wicked desire.   The hordes then went
Before Jericho's bastions,   and the Bairn of the Lord
Was mighty among the multitude.   There men sat by the way;
Blind were they both: they had need of betterment —
Both these blind men   from the Bairn of God,
Since for so long   they had done without light.
They heard the crowd coming   and, most curious, did ask —
That twain wholly blind —   what man, high-born and mighty,
Was the first there   amid the clans of the folk,

The noblest at their head.   Then one hero replied unto
                                them,
Quoth that Jesus Christ there   from Galilee-land,
The Best of all Healers,   was the highest of all:
Foremost was He 'mid His folk.   Full joyous were they of
                                heart,
Both the blind men,   when they knew that God's Bairn,
The Christ, was there 'mid the folk.   They called unto
                        Him with their words:
Loudly they called Holy Christ,   bade that He find them
                                help,
"Master and Liege, David's Son,   be Thou mild unto us
                        with Thy deeds.
Save us from our distress!   As Thou doest for so many
Of the kith of mankind;   Thou art kind to the multitude!
Thou helpest and healest!"   Then the host of the people
With their words began to forbid them   from calling
                        the Wielder,
Lord Christ, so loudly.   But the two listened not,
But ever more and still more   over the crowd of the men
Did they call most loudly.   Christ Healer did stop,
The Best of all Bairns,   hight that they bring them to Him,
Lead them to Him through the land-folk;   and spoke alike
                                wisely
And mildly in front of the many.   "Why seek ye help of
                        Me here?" quoth He.
They bade Him heal them,   bade that He make that their
                        eyen be opened,
That He lend unto them of this light,   that they might
                        see the bustling life
Of the folk, might see   the shining rays of the sun,
This winsome, fair world.   And the Wielder did so.
And with His hands He did touch them;   and He granted
                        His help,
That the eyen be opened   of the blind men twain,
That they might see earth and heaven   through God's holy
                                strength,

The light and the land-folk.   Then they lauded God,
Praised our Lord that they   could enjoy the light of this
day.
And the two went with Him   and followed His tracks.
A favor was theirs; and the Wielder's work   was made widely
known,
And many did marvel.

XLIV

A mighty picture,
A token was shown   there where the blind men sat
By the wayside   and endured wicked pain,
Most bereft of the light: by that are meant the children
of men,
All of mankind;   how Almighty God
In the very beginning   through His own great power
Himself created   that single couple,
Adam and Eve.   He gave them the upward way,
The kingdom of Heaven,   but the hated one was yet near,
The Fiend with his wiles,   and works of wickedness,
With sin he deceived them,   until they forsook it —
the light —
Beauty unending.   They were banished both
To a worse place indeed,   to this mid-world here,
Endured in the darkness   dire human toil,
Won unhappy exile,   lost their worldly goods.
They forgot God's kingdom,   but gave the devils service,
The Fiend's own bairns.   Therefore were they blinded
of heart,
The children of men   in this mid-world here,
Since they would not know Him,   God Mighty and Strong,
The Heavenly Lord,   who with His hands did create them,
Worked them so, as He willed.   So was this world cast
away,
Forced into darkness   and into great despair
And the dale of death.   They did sit along the way

Of the Lord, lamenting of heart,   begging God's help;
But aid could not be granted unto them   before All-
                    Wielding God
Would send unto these   the True Son of Himself:
The Mighty Lord sent Him   to this mid-world here
To make free the light   for the bairns of mankind,
Opening for them eternal life,   so that they could know
The All-Wielding Lord,   the God ever Mighty.
I may eke tell unto you,   if ye are so willed
To hope and to hear,   so that the Healer's, the Savior's
                    strength
Ye may recognize well   how His coming became
Great help to the many   in this mid-world here;
What He, our Master, did mean —   so many a thing
With His acts and His deeds,   and why that well-known town
Is hight Jericho,   the one which standeth there in Judea,
Made well with its walls.   That is named for the moon,
For that bright constellation: it cannot escape its time,
But on every day   it doeth one or the other:
It waneth or waxeth.   So do in the world,
On this mid-earth here,   the bairns of mankind.
They fare forth and follow,   and from them the old die
                    away,
And the young come again and are born.   And the children
                    of men
Wax great until Weird once more   taketh them out of the world.
This the Bairn of God did mean,   as He left the bastions,
The Good Christ from Jericho,   that the children of men
Would not be healed from their blindness,   not see the
                    bright beam
And beauty eternal,   before He Himself had assumed
Man's body and flesh   in this mid-world here.
Then the children of men,   who before sat in sin
And in suffering,   bereft of their sight,
Enduring the darkness —   they did perceive and did know
That to this folk the Healer was come   from the kingdom
                    of Heaven,

Christ the Best of All Kings.   They could soon recognize
                              Him,
Had perceived His path.   Then the people cried out so
                              greatly,
The men to the Mighty God,   that He became mildly inclined,
The Wielder, unto them.   But their wickedness kept them
Most dreadfully, the dire sins,   which once they had
                              done,
Prevented their believing;   but they could not prevent
The will of the people.   For unto All-Wielding God
They did call most loudly,   until He did grant unto them
                              wholeness,
So that they might see   the life never ending,
Eternal light open before them   and journey on
To the bright dwelling above.   So did the blind men mean
Who at Jericho-burg   called to God's Bairn,
Who did cry aloud   that He grant them healing,
Light in this life.   But a great lot of the folk
Who stood in His way,   both before and behind Him,
Kept Him away with their words.   So do those weighted with
                              sin
Unto the kith of mankind   in this mid-world here.
Hear ye now how the blind men acted   after they had been
                              healed,
So that they could see   the light of the sun —
Hear what they then did: they went along with their
                              Master,
Followed in His footsteps,   spoke full many a word,
Lauding the Lord's Herdsman: so do the bairns of the
                              land-folk still
Widely here in this world,   since All-Wielding Christ
Hath illuminated them with His lesson,   granted them
                              light everlasting,
Granted the kingdom of God   to every good man,
The high, heavenly light   and His help to that end
To whosoever worketh   to follow along on His way.

XLV

Then Christ the Savior,   the Good One, soon came
Near to Jerusalem.   And now there approached Him
A great multitude   all of good mind toward Him.
They received Him with joy,   and before Him they strewed
The way with their garments, their weeds;   and with herb-
                    roots,
With bright colored blossoms   and the branches of trees
                    they did strew it,
The field, with fair palms;   and it so then came to pass
That the Son of God   did wish to go
To that most hated town.   Joyous, the multitude
Of the people surrounded Him   and raised songs of praise,
The folk, all willingly: they said thanks to the Wielder
That He Himself was come,   He — Son of David —
To visit the world-folk.   Then Wielding Christ,
The Good, saw Jerusalem.   The Best of All Men
Beheld the town's bastions   and the buildings of Jews,
The high-horned halls   and God's house as well,
The most winsome of temples.   Then within Him welled
His thoughts 'gainst His heart.   And the Holy Bairn
Could not help weeping,   but troubled of heart
With many words He did speak —   for His spirit was
                    sore.
"Woe unto thee, Jerusalem," He wailed,   "that the word
                    of thy Weird
Thou knowest not,   nor what still shall come over thee,
How thou shalt be surrounded   by the strength of a host,
How grim-minded men   shall besiege thee mightily —
The foe with its folk.   For thou shalt never find peace
With these men, or protection.   Many will bring thee
The weapon's point and its edge,   bring thee words of
                    war,
Consume thy folk-clans   with the flames of fire,
Lay waste to thy bailiwicks;   fell these high walls
To the earth itself.   Not a rock will stand upright,

No stone on another.   But all the townships surrounding
Jerusalem will be desolation   for the folk of the Jews,
Since they cannot see   that their time draweth nearer;
But their souls are in doubt,   and they ween not at all,
That the strength of the Wielder   is visited on them."
Then the Lord of Mankind   went with the multitude
Into the bright borough.   When the Bairn of God
Went into Jerusalem   with His host of men,
Was there with His vassals,   there waxed the greatest of
                            all songs:
With such loud voices   they sang holy words.
Lo, the crowds of the folk   did laud the word of the
                            Lord,
The Best of all Bairns.   The burg was astir,
The people were frightened   and asked first of all
Who was that who was come   there with the crowd,
With that multitude great.   Then spoke a man in reply:
Quoth that this was Jesus Christ   from Galilee-land,
Who was come as a Savior   from the city of Nazareth,
Wise Soothsayer and Prophet,   as a Help to the people.
Then the Jews, who had a grudge   against Him already,
Became hate-filled of heart   and hurting of spirit,
Because the people did give   unto Him so much praise,
Did love so their Master.   The dull-minded folk did go forth,
So that they might speak words   with All-Wielding Christ.
Bade that He hight His disciples   be silent here,
Bade Him not to permit them,   the people, to praise Him
So much with their words: "It doth worry this folk,"
                            quoth they,
"These burghers here."   Then again spoke God's Bairn:
"If ye keep the children of men,"   quoth He, Lord Christ,
"From praising with words   the All-Wielder's might,
Then shall the stones   still shout it forth
To the kinship of men,   and the strong, tall cliffs,
Before it is left undone;   but that He shall be lauded
Wide and far in the world."   Then He went into the temple.
He entered God's house.   There He found a horde of the
                            Jews:

There were countless men,   so many together,
Who had chosen for themselves   a selling-place in there,
Haggling o'er multitudes of small matters: and money-
                    changers did sit
Within the temple.   For transactions daily
They held it ready.   Then God's Bairn was enraged,
Drove them out of the temple far;   quoth that it was a
                    far righter deed,
If the children of Israel   should come there to pray:
"And here in this house   let them pray for help,
That the Master of Victories   make them free from sin —
Rather than that thieves   should bargain their things in
                    the house,
And villainous men   make their usurious deals,
The worst of all wrongs.   No whit of honor
Know ye in God's house,   ye folk of the Jews."
So did the Lord All-Powerful   empty and order
The holy house;   and of help this was
To the many of mankind,   who had heard of His might,
Of His strength from afar.   And they came there faring
Over the long, long way.   So many a one weak of limb,
So many of the halt were healed,   and the crippled of
                    hand,
And the blind were made whole.   So did the Bairn of God
Do unto the willing folk,   since He wields might over all,
Over the lives of men   and their lands as well.

XLVI

Before the temple He stood,   Strong Wielding Christ,
The Land-Warder Beloved,   and lo, He took heed
Of the hearts of the people,   and their will; He saw
                    a huge host
Bringing great treasures   to the well-known house,
Giving unto it gold,   goodly webs of silk,
Precious stones and jewels.   Wisely perceived He,
Our Lord Christ, all this.   There did come also a widow,

A poor, ill-weirded woman;   and she went to the altar,
And in that treasure-house   she put down just two
Small coins of bronze;   she was simple of heart,
A woman of good will.   Then spake All-Wielding Christ,
The Man, to His followers;   quoth that a far greater gift
Had she brought to the altar   than any other son of man-
                                                kind.
"If wealthy men," He did tell them,   "bring a treasure-
                                                trove,
An honor here to the house,   still they have left more
                                                at home
Of the wealth they have won.   Not so did this widow,
When she gave all she had upon this altar:
All the wealth she had won.   Not a whit did she leave,
No goods in her garden.   Therefore is her gift more
And worthier to the Wielder,   since she gave with such will
To the house of God.   So shall she receive goodly reward,
Most long-lasting return,   since she possessed such be-
                                                lief."
So I discovered   that All-Wielding Christ
Taught them with words   each day in the temple,
The Master of Mankind.   And many stood 'round Him,
A great folk of the Jews,   and hearkened to the good
                                                word,
The sweet word He spoke.   Some were so blessed,
Some men from the multitude,   that in their minds and
                                                their hearts
They began to learn and accept   the lesson which the
                                                Warder of Lands,
The Child of the Lord,   did speak in His pictures.
To some again the lesson   of Christ was all loathsome,
The All-Wielder's word.   Of hate-willed heart
Were all those who were the greatest   among those governing,
The princes of the people.   These evil men did plan
Trickery and snares with their words;   they had taken
                                                adversaries
To help them,   these men of the highest one;   were thanes
                                                of Herod —

He who was present with an evil intent   to overhear all
they said —
If the people did capture Him,   that they might throw
Him in chains,
Might lay leg-fetters   around His limbs —
Around Him, the Christ without sin.   The crowd did come
toward Him,
Bitter-minded, to speak   unto God's Bairn,
The evil adversaries,   to address Him with words.
"What, Thou art a sayer of law,"   quoth they, "unto all
people?
Thou revealest so wonderous much truth.   Nor is it of
worth unto Thee
To conceal aught from a man   because of his might;
But ever Thou speakest only   that which is right,
And with Thy teaching Thou leadest   the crowds of the
land-folk
Upon God's way. Among the people   not a whit of reproach
Can one find in Thee.   Now we shall ask Thee:
That rich and great ruler —   what right doeth he have?
Caesar from Rome,   who seeketh his tithe
From the clansmen here   and hath counted out
What monies each man   of us shall pay every year,
How much of the head-tax.   Say, what in Thy heart hast
Thou thought?
Is this right or no?   Counsel Thy countrymen well,
For we have need of Thy teachings."   They wanted His
answer,
But well did He know their will.   "Why, ye liars all
Against truth," quoth He,   "do ye tempt Me so boldly?"
But it shall be of no help,   no advantage to you.
That ye deceivers seek   to capture me secretely."
He commanded that they carry forth   the coins for the
showing,
"Which are your duty to give."   The Jews did bring out
A coin of silver;   and many did see
How indeed it was minted;   in the middle appeared

The pictured head of their lord.   Then Holy Christ did
                        question them
As to whose likeness   lay in this picture.
They replied that it was   the world emperor there
From the city of Rome,   "who rules o'er this realm,
Wielding power here in this world."   "That will I verily,"
                        quoth He,
"Say unto you, that ye give   unto him his own,
To the world-lord his wealth,   and to All-Wielding God
Bring that which is His.   That should be your souls,
The spirits of men."   Then the minds of the Jews were made
Small in the gathering.   The scoundrels assembled
Could not win out with their words,   as was indeed their will,
To ensnare Him,   since the Peace-Bairn of God
Warded off their wickedness,   and He verily
Said unto them a soothy thing;   still they were not so
                        blessed,
That they could receive it   and it could then be of bene-
                        fit unto them.

                        XLVII

But they would not leave off,   but instead ordered a woman
                        led forth
In front of the crowd;   she had committed sin,
Had truly done wrong;   the woman had been taken
In adultery   and had forfeited her life,
So that the bairns of mankind   could deprive her of
                        breath —
Lay claim to her age: for so was the law.
They began to question Him;   the bold people there —
Wicked they with their words: what they should do with
                        this wife:
Whether to kill her by torment   or leave her quick and
                        alive —
Or what judgment He would deal   for such a deed as this.
"Thou wist," quoth they, "that Moses   commanded these many

With words of truth   that any woman whosoever
Is found in adultery   must forfeit her life,
And that with their hands the landsmen   will unlife her
By throwing sharp stones.   Now Thou mayest see her here
                 standing,
Ensnared in her sin: say what Thou willst!"
His foes had the wish   to ensnare Him with words.
If He were to say that they   should indeed let her live,
Should permit her to leave here in peace,   then would the
                 people of Jews
Say that He had opposed   their ancient law,
The people's own land-right.   If He hight them rob her of
                 life,
The maid before the many;   then would they say that no
                 mildness of heart
He bore in His breast,   such as God's Bairn should in-
                 deed possess.
So for whichever word   Holy Christ would speak
To the people, the many,   they would then punish Him,
Would deal out His doom.   This our Lord Christ did perceive.
Right well did He know   the turn of mind of these men,
Their wicked wills,   when He spoke then to the folk,
To all the earls gathered around.   "Which of you," quoth He
"Standeth here without evil sin?   Let him himself go to
                 her
And with his hands be the first   of the earls here
To pelt her with stones."   Then the Jews stood about,
Had their thoughts and were silent.   Not a single thane
Could find opposition   unto this speech.
And each man was reminded   of his own evil-mindedness,
Of his own dark sins;   not a one was sure enough
That after this word   he would venture to throw
A stone against the woman;   but they left her standing
                 alone inside.
The grim-minded people   of the Jews did go thence,
One after another,   until there was not a single one
Of the folk of the foe   standing before them

Who would have wanted to rob   this woman of her years
                    and her life.
Then I discovered that the Peace Bairn of God,   the Best of
                    all Men,
Did question her. "Whence came   this Jewish folk?" quoth
                    He,
"Thy opponents here,   who have accused thee to Me —?
Those who today have wanted   to torment thee most terribly,
To bereave thee of life —   have they done one whit of harm
                    unto thee?"
Then the woman gave answer   again unto Him,
Quoth that through the holy help   of the Savior no one had
                    harmed her
To reward her sins.   Then spake again All-Wielding Christ,
The Master of Mankind.   "Nor shall I do harm unto thee,"
                    He made reply,
"But go thou hence, hale   and unhurt, and let it be
The care of thy heart,   that henceforth thou sinnest no
                    more."
The Holy Bairn of the Lord   had helped her indeed,
Had protected her life.   Then the people of Jews stood
                    there,
As bent on evil,   as they had been in the beginning,
Of wicked intent and wanting   to continue their word-strife,
Pondering, how to pursue it   with the Peace-Bairn of God.
They had put doubts in the faith   of the people:
The little folk standing about   would far liefer
Have accomplished His will,   the word of God's Bairn,
Have done even so,   as their Lord did bid them.
They strove toward right   better than those men with
                    riches,
Held Him as their Lord;   yea, as the Heaven-King even,
And followed Him gladly.   Then God's Son did go
Within the temple.   The people surrounded Him truly,
The multitude of the men.   He stood in their midst,
Taught them, the land-folk,   with words of light
And in a voice loud and bright: there was great listening,

And many a thane stood silent;   and He bade them thusly:
"Whosoever of the people   be oppressed with thirst —
Let him come unto Me,"   quoth He, "and drink every day
From that sweet spring.   So may I say unto you,
Whosoever of the bairns of mankind   hath believed in Me
Fast and firmly among the folk —   that from him shall flow
The living flood,   flow from his body
The gushing water,   the great well-springs
That are springs of life coming thence.   This word
                              shall come true,
Shall be done unto all folk,   whosoever hath believed
                        rightly in Me."
With this water   All-Wielding Christ,
The High King of Heaven   did mean the Holy Ghost,
How the children of men   should receive Him,
Light and reason   and the life everlasting,
The high kingdom of Heaven   and Holy God's grace.

XLVIII

Then the people began to quarrel   about the teachings
                              of Christ
And about His words;   haughty men stood about,
Proud minded Jews —   and they spoke much mockery,
Heaped scorn upon Him,   saying that they could hear full
                        well
That angry and wicked thought   did speak out of Him.
"Now He doth teach evil,"   quoth they, "with every word."
And again others did speak: "Ye should not reproach
Him who teacheth," quoth they,   "for words of life come
Mighty out of His mouth,   and He worketh many a thing,
Many a wonder here in this world: that is no wicked deed,
Clearly not the might of the Fiend,   else could not such
                        good be accomplished by Him,
But surely it cometh   from All-Wielding God,
From His strength all rightly.   That may ye well recognize
In His words of truth,   that He wieldeth power

Over all the earth."   Then His opposers longed
To take Him captive straightway   or to cast stones on Him,
Had they not feared there   the multitude of the folk,
Been afraid of the people.   Then spoke the Peace Bairn
                    of God.
"Much good have I shown unto you,"   quoth He, "from God
                    Himself,
Both in words and in works.   Now would ye give me wicked
                    reward
With your strong, hard hearts   and pelt me with stones
And bereave me of life."   Then again the people replied,
His dire opponents: "We do this   not because of Thy deeds,"
                    quoth they,
"That we should want   to deprive Thee of life.
But we do so because of Thy words,   since Thou speakest
                    such wickedness,
Since Thou dost praise Thyself   and sayest such blasphemy,
Proclaiming before these Jews   that Thou art God Himself,
The Mighty Master and Lord;   and Thou art merely a man
                    like us,
Art come from these clans."   Then All-Wielding Christ
No longer wished to list   to the scorn of the Jews,
The will of these wicked ones.   But from the temple He went
Over Jordan's stream.   His disciples He had with Him,
Those blessed thanes,   who forever there tarried
To accomplish His will.   Another folk He did seek;
The Lord Himself did work there,   as was ever His wont,
Teaching the land-folk: those who so wanted belief
In His Holy word.   Each man should well do so ever
If he accepteth and receiveth   it into his heart.
Then I did hear there were come   to Holy Christ
Heralds from Bethany,   and they said unto God's Bairn
That women had sent them   there on this errand —
Mary and Martha,   maidens most comely,
Such winsome women.   Both He knew well.
They were sisters twain,   whom in His spirit
He Himself did love   for their mildness of heart,

These women for their goodly will.   Most verily they sent
From Bethany for Him;   for their brother was bedfast —
Lazarus he —   and they feared for his life.
They bade that He come,   All-Wielding Christ,
The Holy, to help them.   As soon as He heard them
Speak about the sick man,   He gave answer straightway,
Said that Lazarus' sickness,   though so serious it was,
Would not do him to death.   "But," He did say, "the love
                    of the Lord
Shall here be accomplished.   Nor shall any harm come unto
                    him
The Son of the Lord   did Himself stay there
Two nights and two days.   The time then drew near,
That He teach these people   the power He had,
Teach the Jewish folk   there in Jerusalem.
Then the Son of the Lord   did say to His thanes
That He would again seek out the Jews   across the Jordan.
But His disciples   did speak to Him in reply:
"For what reason, good Master,   goest Thou so gladly,"
Quoth they, "over there?   Was it not recently there,
That they thought to kill Thee   because of Thy words?
Did want to pelt Thee with strong, sharp stones?   Now
                    Thou strivest to go again,
Among that fight-seeking folk.   Thou hast foes enough,
Overhaughty earls."   Then one of the twelve,
Thomas, did speak —   he was truly an excellent man,
A loyal thane of his Lord.   "Let us never reproach His deeds,"
Quoth he, "nor reproach His will.   But rather we should
                    remain with Him,
Should suffer with our Lord.   For that is the choice of
                    a thane:
That he standeth steadfast   with his Liege together,
Doth die with Him at his doom.   Let us all do so there-
                    fore;
Let us follow His path,   nor let our lives
Be worth aught against His,   unless we may die
In this host with our Lord.   So honor will live after us,

A good word before the kinships of men." So the disciples
                              of Christ,
The aethling-born earls, became all of one mind,
Holding the will of their Lord. Then Holy Christ Himself
Did say to His disciples, that a sleep unto death
Lay on Lazarus on his couch. "He hath given up the
                              light,
Doth slumber on, on his bedstead. Now we shall fare on
                              the way
To awaken him there, so that he may again see this world
Alive, see the light: Then your belief will henceforth
Be strengthened still more. So went He hence o'er the
                              flood;
The Good Son of God did go with His vassals
There to Bethany — the Bairn of the Lord
Himself with His disciples — there where the sisters
                              twain,
Mary and Martha, their minds filled with care,
Were sitting most sadly. Here was gathered together
Much folk of the Jews from Jerusalem,
Who wanted to comfort the women with words,
So that they would lament less the death of Lazarus,
The loss of the child-young man. Then as the Warder of
                              Lands
Did go through the garden, it spread around that God's
                              Bairn
Had now arrived, and that He, so mighty,
Did tarry outside the castle. Then the twain, the women,
Were most joyous indeed, when they heard that the Wielder,
The Peace-Bairn of God, was now come unto them.

XLIX

'Twas the most wonderous joy for the woman to hear
Of the Lord's coming and of the word of Christ.
Her mind filled with care, Mary did go to the One so
                              Mighty,

137

Lamenting, exchanged words   and spoke with the Wielder,
Her heart muchly troubled.   "Had you, my Master,"
Quoth she, "been nearer,   O Best of Saviors,
Healer so good, I would never   have needed to suffer
                                 such hurt,
Such bitter care in my breast,   and my brother would not
                                 now be dead,
Lazarus, far from the light;   but he would still be alive,
Filled with this life.   But I, my Lord, do believe
Most steadfastly in Thee,   Thou Best of all Teachers.
If Thou would'st so bid   the Bright Lord for aught,
He would grant it straightway;   Almighty God
Would fulfill Thy will."   Then spoke again All-Wielding
                                 Christ,
Answering the woman.   "Let not thy heart within thee"
Quoth He, "become darkened,   but I may make known unto thee
In words of truth, that thou   shalt have neither worry
                                 nor doubt,
But that thy brother shall   at the bidding of God,
Through the might of the Lord   arise from the dead
In his own body itself."   "So have I believed, " quoth she,
That it will thus come to pass   when the world doth end,
That he shall arise   then again from the earth
On the day of his doom: then the dead will become quick
Through the might of the Lord;   and so many of mankind
Will arise from their rest."   Then Christ the Ruler did
                                 speak,
The Almighty did utter   open words to the women;
That He Himself   was the Son of the Lord,
For the bairns of mankind   both a light and a life
For the resurrection.   "Never shall he die,
Take leave of this life,   who believeth in Me.
Though the bairns of men   do bury him deeply
And cover him over with earth,   he is not yet dead:
The flesh is consigned to the soil,   but the spirit is saved,
And the soul is still sound."   Then the good wife again did
                                 speak

138

To Him with Her words: "I verily believe," quoth she,
"That Thou art the Christ, the Son of God.   Well may one
                    see this,
May know from Thy words   that Thou wieldest power
Through this holy creation   over heaven and earth."
Then I discovered that   the other woman did come,
Mary, with care-filled mind: and behind her came many
Of the folk of the Jews gathered together.   And to the
                    Bairn of God
She, saddened of spirit, did say,   why she was sorrowed
With such grief in her heart;   she lamented with groans
The losing of Lazarus,   of the beloved man,
Giving forth mournful moans,   until the Almighty's Bairn
Was indeed moved in His heart;   and hot tears streamed,
Welling up as He wept.   And to the woman He spoke,
Hight that they should lead Him,   there where Lazarus
                    was lying
Consigned to the soil.   A stone lay above him;
A hard boulder did cover him.   The Holy Christ hight
Them remove the rock so that   right well He might see
                    the corpse,
Might gaze on the body.   Then despite the folk gathered
                    'round,
Mary could not help making known   the care of her mind, and
                    to the Mighty One
She did speak, "My Lord so Good," quoth she,   "if one taketh
                    away the stone,
Removeth this rock, then I ween,   it will reek from there.
An unsweet stench will come forth,   if I may so say
Unto Thee with words of truth —   that there is no doubt of
                    that —
Four days and four nights hath it been,   since he was consigned
To his grave there."   He gave reply unto her,
The All-Wielder unto the woman.   "Why, I have verily told
                    thee before, "quoth He,
"If thou hast will to believe,   then will it not be long
Before thou shalt see, shalt know   the strength of the
                    Lord,

The great might of God.   Then many did go
And hove up the hard stone.   Then Holy Christ did gaze
Upward with His eyes   and said thanks unto Him
Who had shaped this world.   "Since Thou hearest My word,"
                    quoth He,
"Thyself Lord of Victory,   I will know that Thou doest so
                    ever.
But I do so only   for the great folk of the Jews,
That they may verily know   that Thou hast sent Me into
                    this world
To teach them, this land-folk."   Then He called unto
                    Lazarus
With a loud, strong voice   and hight him stand up
And go forth from the grave.   And his ghost did return
And enter his body.   And he began moving his limbs:
He stirred 'neath his weeds;   but he was still wound in them,
Held tight by his shroud.   Then All-Wielding Christ did
                    hight
That they give him help.   Then the men did go
And unwound his weeds.   Winsome, he rose,
Lazarus to this light.   His life had been granted him,
So that he might spend   the fated span of his days
Henceforth in peace.   The twain rejoiced full well,
Mary and Martha;   nor may anyone
Truly say otherwise   than that the sisters twain
Were indeed happy of heart.   Many did wonder,
Those of the Jewish folk,   when they did see him
Rise sound from his grave —   him, whom sickness had taken
                    before
And whom they had dug   deep down into the earth,
Him, cut loose from his life.   Henceforth he could live
Hale and sound in his home.   So may the Heaven-King's,
May God's great power   protect the life
Of so many a man,   and may help him 'gainst the hate
Of the Fiend — Holy God,   to whomsoever He giveth His
                    grace.

140

L

Then the minds of so many   of mankind and their thoughts
                as well
Were won for the Christ,   when they themselves did see
His holy works,   since in this world such wonders
Had never before come to pass.   There were also some
                people,
Such strong-minded men —   the might of God they had no will
To acknowledge openly,   but against His great power
They fought with their words: for the Wielder's message,
His lesson, was so loathsome to them,   that they sought
                other landsmen
In Jerusalem —   there where the Jews
Had their home and inheritance,   their foremost town —
There they gathered a great crowd   of grim-minded folk,
And of Christ's work they did tell them;   quoth that they
                had seen him quick
And alive — with their own eyes had seen   the earl who
                had been in the earth,
Consigned to a grave   four nights and four days,
Had been dead and buried,   until He with His deeds,
With His words had awakened Him   to see this world once
                again.
This was so hateful   to these haughty men,
To the clansmen of Jews,   that they commanded their minions,
Their people to gather together   and to turn the crowd
Against Him — the great host;   and against Mighty Christ
They took counsel in whispers;   "That is not good advice,"
                quoth they,
"That we should endure it.   Too many indeed of the folk
Believe in His lessons.   Then the landsmen will come
And attack us with horsemen,   and our overseers
Will be warriors from Rome.   Then bereft of our realm,
Must we live and suffer   the loss of our lives,
We heroes, the loss of our heads.   Then spoke a hoary man
Over the crowd of the men: among the clans

Within the borough   was he bishop of the people.
Kaiphas was he called,   and by the kinsmen of Jews
He had been chosen this year   to take charge of God's
                    house,
Be the warder, then, of the temple.   "Methinks 'tis a
                    wonder," said he,
"O praiseworthy people —   ye are informed of a plenty:
Why is it that ye yet do not know,   O ye folk of the
                    Jews,
That 'tis better counsel   for the bairns of mankind
That one relieve   one man of his life
And that he dieth   most bloodily through your deeds,
Forsaketh this life   for the folk-clans here,
Than that all the landsmen   should forever be lost."
But it was not *his* will   that he verily did speak
Forth to the land-folk   for the weal of mankind,
Proclaimed to the people;   but from God's power it came
Through his holy office,   since he had to care for God's
                    house
In Jerusalem there —   he, the temple's warder.
Therefore the people's bishop did speak,   how the Bairn
                    of God
Was to save all the children   of earth with His single
                    spirit,
With His own very life: and for all the land-folk
That was a great gain,   for He gathered the heathen,
All-Wielding Christ fetched   the men, as He willed.
Then those most haughty men   became of one mind,
The clansmen of Jews,   and in their crowd they did speak —
This far-known people,   that they permit no doubt in their
                    minds!
But whosoever might find Him   here among the folk —
He should straightway make Him   his captive, should bring
                    Him
Forth to the diet of clans;   quoth that they no longer
                    cared
To suffer that *one* man   should thus seduce them,

142

The world-folk all.   But All-Wielding Christ knew full well
Even the thoughts in the minds   of these men there,
Their hate-angry hearts;   for nothing is ever hidden
To Him in this mid-world here;   thereafter He had no wish
To appear in the open   among the many, among the earls
Of the folk, among the Jews.   For the Son of God
Was biding that bright, glorious time   which would be unto
                    Him,
When He would endure great pain   for these peoples,
Torment indeed for the folk of the earth.   For the time of
                    His doom
He knew full well.   Thereupon our Lord went forth.
All-Wielding Christ   did abide in Ephraim.
The Holy Lord did   dwell in the high-walled city
With His vassals there;   until it was His will
To return to Bethany once more   with His mighty host,
With His disciples good.   The Jews did discuss
His every word: "This bodeth no good," quoth they,
"For the council of our realm.   Though we do speak rightly,
Still our cause cannot thrive one whit,   since He can
                    turn them,
The folk to His will;   and all the world followeth Him,
The landsmen for His lesson,   so that we may do no whit
Of harm unto Him,   here in front of the folk."

                    LI

Thus the Bairn of God   did go into Bethany
Six nights before it should hap —   that gathering there
In Jerusalem   of the Jewish folk.
For the hallowed day   they should keep for the holy tide,
The Passover of Jews.   God's Son did tarry
Mighty among the many.   A great crowd of men,
Of folk did wait for His words.   There two women approached
                    Him,
Mary and Martha;   with mildness of spirit
They served Him most humbly.   The Master of Peoples

Gave them long-lasting reward.　　He released them from all
　　　　　　　　that is loathsome,
Absolved them from sin;　　and He Himself did bid
That they should fare forth　　in peace against the Foe,
The women with His good permission;　　To His will had they
　　　　　　　　turned
Ever their service.　　Then All-Wielding Christ
Fared forth with His people,　　the Lord of the Folk,
To Jerusalem,　　where dwelt the Jews,
All those hate-filled leaders,　　who there spent the holy
　　　　　　　　time
Warding the temple.　　There were there many world-folk
Of most mighty clans;　　and they cared not to hear
The word of the Christ,　　nor had they a whit
Of love in their breasts　　for the Bairn of God;
But rather they were a proud,　　a wrath-filled people,
An angry minded clan of mankind;　　and they had murderous
　　　　　　　　thoughts
And evil within them:　　all wrongly they understood
The teachings of Christ,　　wanted to kill Him, the All-
　　　　　　　　Strong,
Because of His words.　　But there were so many of the world-
　　　　　　　　folk,
So many of the earlships　　about Him all the day long.
The small folk did surround Him　　for the sake of His
　　　　　　　　sweet word,
With so many people all the day,　　so that His enemies
Among the folk-clans　　feared to make Him their captive,
Avoiding Him there amid the many.　　Now Mighty Christ
Did stand inside of the temple　　and said many a word
All the day long,　　until the light,
Till the sun went to rest.　　Then many did wend their way
Homeward, that kith of mankind.　　There was there a famous
　　　　　　　　mountain
Outside near the city —　　so broad it was and so high,
Green and so fair:　　it was hight by the Jewish folk
The Mountain of Olives.　　Upon that did He go,

The Savior Christ,   where the night did surround Him.
He was there with His disciples,   though not one of the
                              Jews
Did actually know this,   since already He had entered the
                              temple —
The Lord of the Land-folk —   when the light came up from
                              the east,
Received the clanships   and said much unto them
In words of truth,   so that not one in this world,
On this mid-earth here —   not a single man is so wise,
Not one of the bairns of mankind,   that he could repeat
                              to the end
All the teachings He told   in the temple there,
Did speak in the holy house;   and with His words He hight
                              them
To make themselves ready   for the realm of God,
All men everywhere whosoever they be,   so that on that
                              best-known day
They may receive   the love of their Lord.
He told them the sins they had committed   and straightway
                              commanded
That they atone for their deeds.   Told them that in their
                              hearts
They should love God's light   and leave behind them all
                              wrongs,
Evil haughtiness,   and assume humility,
And take it into their hearts.   Quoth that the kingdom of
                              Heaven,
The richest of goods was really for them.   Then right many
                              of the men
Were turned to His will,   when they heard God's word,
Heard the Holy Message   of the King of Heaven,
Acknowledged great power   and the Master's coming
And the help of the Lord;   yea, that the heavenly kingdom,
That salvation was grown nearer,   and the grace of God
For the bairns of mankind.   But some were so angered —
Some of the Jewish folk   had such grimness of mind,

Such hate-filled hearts...[1]
They wanted not to believe His word,   but waged great
                              battle
Against Christ's might: because of their wretched contention
The folk could not find it —   belief in Him, clear and firm.
The grace was not granted them   to be given the kingdom of
                              Heaven.
Then God's Son did go,   and His disciples all gladly with
                              Him;
The Wielder went from the temple,   as He so willed it.
And again the Bairn of God   did go up on the mountain,
And He sat with His disciples   and said much unto them
In words of truth.   They began to talk with Him about the
                              temple,
The men about God's house,   quoth that no goodlier
Building had ever been builded   by the hands of earls,
By the efforts of man,   never such temple erected
With such great power.   Then the Rich Prince did speak,
The High King of Heaven —   and the others did hear Him —
"I can yet tell unto you," quoth He,   "that the time shall
                              soon come
That no stone shall be left   standing upon any other,
But it shall fall to the earth   and fire shall devour it,
The greedy flames,   though it be so goodly,
So wisely worked. And that   is the Weird of the world:
The green meads shall all pass away."   Then His followers
                              did go to Him,
And they asked Him softly: "How long shall it stand here?"
                              quoth they,
"The world in its winsomeness,   before the great turning
                              will come,
Until the last day   of light shineth through
Its covering of clouds;   or when can we hope for Thy coming
To this mid-world again   to judge mankind and its dead
                              and its quick,

[1] Lacuna in MS.

146

O my Lord most Good?   We have longing to know,
O All-Wielding Christ,   when that time shall come."

LII

Then All-Wielding Christ   did give answer,
The Goodly Man,   Himself, to the many.
"That hath the Good Lord   so hidden," quoth He
"The Father of Heaven's kingdom   hath so concealed it,
The Wielder over the World,   so that not a one
Of the children of men can tell   when this noted time
Shall come to the world;   nor in truth can they know
Either, God's angels,   who are ever beside Him
And stand in His sight,   nor can they say it,
With their words tell   all truly, when it shall hap,
That from the mid-world here   the Mighty Lord
Shall choose to call   the children of men. He alone
knows,
The Father, Holy in Heaven.   From all others 'tis hidden:
From the quick and the dead,   when that coming shall be.
Yet may I tell unto you   what wonderous token
Shall happen here   before He shall come to this world
On that famous day.   For it shall be revealed in the
moon
And in the sun as well;   both shall turn swarthy,
Be surrounded in darkness,   and the stars shall fall,
The white, heavenly beacons;   this broad earth shall
tremble,
This wide world shake.   And many such signs shall there
be:
The great sea shall rage grimly   and the ocean tide grow
To bring dread with its waves   to the dwellers of earth.
Mankind will shrivel and die   in its mighty distress.
People will pass away in their fears;   and in no place
will there be peace.
But wars so many   will rise over the earth,
Filled with hatred all;   and one clan shall lead a host

Against another.   The battle of kings will arise,
Mighty wanderings of hosts: and many a murder will there
                              be —
There open war-death — that is a terrible thing
That man should ever   commit such murders.
Great ruination will spread awide   over all the world —
The most farflung dying of men   that was ever upon this
                              mid-earth here
Through plagues and through pestilence.   People lie sick;
They do drop and they die;   and their day endeth.
With their life they fulfill it;   a famine immeasurable,
A grim, hot hunger fares   huge o'er the bairns of all men,
The greatest of starving;   and that is not the slightest
Of the torments which shall hap   here in this world
Before the day of all doom.   Whenever ye see such deeds
Being done in this world,   then may ye verily know
That the last day draweth nigh   for the land-folk all,
That most noted day,   and the might of God
And the stirring of heavenly strength   and the Savior's
                              coming,
The Lord's, in His glory.   Lo, for these deeds
Ye may know a token   in the very trees:
When they make buds and bloom   and show forth leaf-blades,
When they unfold their foliage,   the children of men may
                              know full well
That soon after this   the summer draweth near,
The warm and the winsome,   and the weather is fair:
So know ye also by this token   which I have told unto you,
When the last day of life   draweth near for the land-
                              folk.
Now will I say unto you   most verily that this folk,
This people shall not pass away   before this be fulfilled
And My word becometh truth.   Yet cometh the turning
Of heaven and earth,   and My Holy Word standeth
In firmness henceforth,   and all will be so fulfilled,
Come to pass in this light,   as I have said to these
                              people.

Verily, wake ye all: for the well-known day,
The day of your doom cometh most certainly,   and so doeth
            the strength,
The might immense of your Lord,   and that most known of
            times,
The turn of this world.   Against this be ye watchful,
That He find you not suddenly asleep   and stretched out
On a couch of ease   with all of your evil deeds,
And filled with your sins.   For the reckoning day
Doth come in the deep, dark night,   as doeth a thief
Furtively all with his deeds: so fareth that day to man-
            kind,
The last of this light,   so that the land-folk know it
            not before,
Even as was the flood   once in former days,
Which destroyed mankind   with its streams of water
In the time of Noah;   but now God saved him only,
Him with his family,   the Holy Lord,
From the flood's fierce onslaught;   so did come also
            the fire
Hot down from heaven   which surrounded the cities
Around Sodom-land,   as swarthy flames,
Greedy indeed and grim,   so that no man did go forth
Still alive except Lot alone;   him the Lord's angels
Did lead from there   with his daughters twain
High onto a mountain;   all others, both land and landsmen,
The burning fire,   the flames destroyed.
So suddenly did come the fire,   and so also was the flood
            before:
So, too, shall be the end-day of earth.   All men whosoever
Should think ahead toward this thing.   That is a great need
For every man; there let each keep   this care firm in his
            heart."

LIII

"When ever it shall come to pass,   that All-Wielding Christ,

Man's Glorious Son,   shall come with God's might,
Shall come with the strength   of the Richest of Kings,
Sit on high in His own great might;   and together with
                    Him,
All the angels, too,   which are above holy in Heaven;
Then shall the children of men   and with them the heathen
Come all together;   all the living kith of the land-folk
                    come,
Whosoever was born, hath lived   here indeed in this light
Of the children of men.   To all of mankind,
To the folk here all,   shall the Lord Most Famous
Deal judgments, as were their deeds.   The doomed men He
                    shall sort out,
The sinful, the lost men,   to his left hand;
So He shall place the holy and blessed   on His right side
                    also,
Greeting the good then   and speaking most gladly to them:
"Come ye," quoth He, "Ye who are chosen,   and receive ye
                    the good kingdom,
The mighty, which standeth ready,   made for the children of
                    men
From the world's beginning.   The Father of Mankind's Bairns
Himself hath hallowed it;   ye may enjoy its blessings,
Rule o'er this wide realm;   since right often ye accom-
                    plished My will,
Followed Me gladly,   and were mild in your giving,
When I was plagued here   with hunger and thirst,
Surrounded by frost;   when I lay fettered
And oppressed in prison;   oft there came to Me in My pain
Help from your hands: ye were mild in your hearts
And visited Me worthily."   Then verily the crowd addressed
                    Him again.
"My Lord most Good," quoth they.   "When didst Thou lan-
                    guish in chains,
Oppressed by such needs,   as Thou now tellest these
                    people,
As Thou, Mighty Master, dost mention?   When hath any man
                    seen Thee

Oppressed by such needs?   Why, Thou hast power over all
                peoples,
Over all treasures as well,   whatever the children of men
Have won in this world.   Then spoke All-Wielding God to
                them once again.
"Whatever ye have done here,"   quoth He, "In the name of
                your Lord,
In honor of God,   have given of your goods
To the men who are the least of those   standing here 'mid
                the many,
To such persons indeed   poor for their humbleness,
Since they accomplished My will —   whatsoever ye gave unto
                them of your wealth,
Ye have done for honor of Me.   Your Lord Himself hath re-
                ceived it,
The help did come to the Heaven-King.   Therefore the Holy
                Lord
Will reward your belief: He giveth life everlasting unto
                you."
Then the Wielder, the Lord,   will turn to those at His
                left hand,
To those men, who are damned,   saying that they must pay
                for their deeds,
These folk for their wrongs;   "Now shall ye fare
From Me," quoth He,   "accursed to eternal fire,
Fare to the fire made ready   for foes of the Lord,
For the folk of the Fiend   for their foul works of sin,
Since ye have not helped Me,   when hunger and thirst
Did torment Me most terribly;   tortured My mind,
I went without clothing: so great was My need,
For I had naught of help   when I was held bound,
Locked into limb-fetters,   and lay taken in illness,
By serious plagues;   for in My sickness ye never
Did will to visit Me —   nor was I of such worth unto you,
That ye thought of Me ever.   Therefore will ye suffer
In hell in the darkness there."   Then the horde of the
                people again spoke to Him:

"Well, All-Wielding God," quoth they,   "Why wilt Thou
              speak so 'gainst the folk?
Say such words 'gainst the many?   When hast Thou ever had
              need of men
Or of the goods of mankind?   Through Thy giving alone do
              they own it,
The wealth of this world."   Then All-Wielding God speaketh
              again.
"When ye have scorned," quoth He,   "the poorest of the
              children of earth,
The least among men;   have considered little
These men in your hearts;   in your hearts have let them
              be hated,
Have denied them your love: then ye did likewise unto
              your Lord,
Denied Him your wealth;   therefore All-Wielding God,
Your Father, refuseth to take you;   but ye must fare into
              the fire,
Go down into the deep death   and there serve the devil,
The evil Fiend,   since thus ye acted before."
After these words He parted   the people in twain,
The good and the evil;   and the damned ones did go
Down into hot hell —   they were troubled of heart —
There they were punished,   received pain never ending,
These men who were damned.   He doth lead them thence,
The High King of Heaven,   leadeth the purified host
Into long-lasting light —   there is life everlasting:
God's realm is made ready   for all of the good.

LIV

So I found out that with His words   the All-Wielding God
Did tell unto His warriors   about the turn of the world,
How it fareth on,   as long as the bairns of the folk
May dwell therein,   but how in the end it shall
Glide away and be lost.   He also said unto His disciples
In words of truth: "Why, ye all wit," quoth He,

"That two nights from today   the time will come,
The paschaltide of the Jews,   when the people must serve
                        their God,
These men in the temple.   It cannot be turned aside,
That the Son of Man be sold   to the multitude,
Full of strength though He be;   and be struck to the cross,
Enduring tortures most monsterious."   Many thanes were
                    there, too — men
From the south gathered together,   a grim-minded folk,
Clanships of Jews   who were come to give service to God.
Those learned in writing,   the rabbis were come
Among the crowd of the men: there were considered the
                        wisest
Among the multitude   of mankind assembled,
A strong clanship.   There was Kaiphas, too —
Bishop was he among the folk.   They spake about God's Bairn,
How they would slay Him,   who was free from sin,
Told how they could not   touch Him on this holy day
Among the multitude of the men,   "Lest the many people,
The hordes be aroused,   since the host is willing
To stand and to battle for Him.   In stillness we should
Entrap Him, His life,   so that the folk of the Jews
Will not rise up   in rebellion on this holy day."
Then Judas came forward to him,   the disciple of Christ,
One of the twelve,   to where the aethlings did tarry,
The clanships of Jews;   quoth that he indeed
Could give them good counsel,   "What will ye pay me?"
                    quoth he,
"What treasure, reward,   if I should turn that Man over
                    to you
Without rebellion or battle?"   Then the hearts of the men
                    became
Joyous, those of the folk: "If thou would'st do so,"
                    quoth they,
"And keep well thy word,   then hast thou the right
To ask for whatsoever   of goodly wealth
Thou dost wish from this folk."   Then the men who were
                    there

Put at his disposal   pieces of silver,
Thirty together;   and he to the gathering did speak
Insolent words: that for this   he would yield his Master
                    unto them.
Then he turned from the men;   evil of mind was he, and
                    disloyal.
He did calculate   when the time would come unto him,
That he might betray Him   to the evil men,
To the folk of the foe.   For the Peace-Bairn of God,
The True Wielding Christ well knew   He must leave this
                    world,
Give up the dwellings of men   and return to the realms of
                    God,
Fare to the ancient fief   of His Father. Never have
The children of men seen more love   than He bore to those
                    men,
To His disciples good.   He prepared a guest meal for them
And sweetly did bid them sit,   and said unto them
Many a word most true.   The day strode to the west,
The sun to its setting.   Then He Himself did bid them,
The Wielder with His words,   that they bring Him water,
For His hands clear water;   and there the Holy Christ did
                    rise
At the feast, the Good Lord,   and the feet of His followers
He washed with His hands,   and wiped them thereafter with
                    towels,
Dried them most carefully.   Then unto his Lord Christ
Simon Peter did speak.   "Methinks 'tis no seemly thing,"
                    quoth he,
"For Thee, my Master so Good,   that Thou shouldst be
                    washing my feet
With those, Thy most holy hands."   The Lord gave reply unto
                    him,
The Wielder then with His words.   "If thou hast not the
                    will," quoth He,
"To accept this thing,   that I wash thy feet
With such love indeed,   as I do for the others,

154

These men, through My love,   then mayest thou not share
                        with Me
The kingdom of Heaven."   His heart was then changed
For Simon Peter.   "Thou Thyself wieldest power," said he,
"My Lord so good,   lo, over my feet and my hands
And my head as well,   to wash them all with Thy hands,
O Ruler, if henceforth   I may have Thy grace
And such part of Thy kingdom   of Heaven as Thou, Lord
                        Christ,
Would'st grant unto me   in Thy goodness."
The disciples of Christ,   those earls, suffered His
                        service
With patience, those thanes,   whatsoever Mighty Christ,
Their Liege, would do unto them,   out of love, and He
                        thought to do
A thing even greater for the children of men.

LV

            The Peace-Child of God
Did go to sit once again   among the people and gave unto
                        them
Much long-lasting counsel.   Then was the light come,
The morning come to mankind.   Almighty Christ
Then greeted His subjects   and asked them where they in-
                        tended
To prepare for the feast   on this festive day,
Where He would hold, would keep   this holy tide
Himself with His disciples.   Then He hight them, His men,
Seek out Jerusalem: "When ye come there," quoth He,
"Within the city itself,   there will be great confusion,
A mighty seething of men —   ye will see a man
Carrying there in his hand   a cup of clear water.
We shall follow him   into whatsoever garden ye do see
                        him go;
And unto that lord   who owneth this house
Ye yourselves shall say   that I have sent you hence

To make ready My feast.   Then will he show you
A goodly house,   a high upper hall
Hung over with brightest array.   There shall ye busy
Yourselves with My meal.   There I shall most certainly
                              come,
Myself and My disciples, too."   Then straightway there-
                              after
The servants of Christ   set out on the way to Jerusalem,
And they did find there   all things even as He had said
With true word-tokens.   Nor was aught truly changed.
They made ready the feast there,   and right soon the Son
                              of God,
The Holy Christ   was come to the house
Where they should accomplish   the custom there of the
                              land,
Following the bidding of God,   as it was for the Jewish
                              folk
Ancient custom and law   from time immemorial.
On the evening   All-Wielding Christ did go
To take His seat in the hall;   and He bade His disciples
Come unto Him, the twelve   who were truest to Him,
These men most loyal   to Him in their minds
Both in words and in ways.   Well did He know
The thoughts in their hearts,   our Holy Lord —
He greeted them over the banquet.   "I yearn indeed,"
He said, "to sit   together with you
And partake of the feast,   share the Passover
Of Jews with you, My beloved.   Now must I tell unto you
The will of the Lord,   that in this world no longer
May I enjoy meat with mankind   before it must be fulfilled,
The kingdom of Heaven.   For Me there is at hand
Both torment and torture,   which I must truly endure
For the people, this land-folk here."   So did He speak to
                              His thanes,
The Holy Lord,   and His heart was grieved,
His spirit darkend with sorrow,   and to His disciples
                              He spoke,

The Good Man to His faithful: "Why, I give unto you the
                    kingdom of God,
Give you the light of Heaven,   and ye give unto Me
Most sweetly your thaneship.   But now ye wish not to ful-
                    fill this,
But waver far from the word.   Now verily I say unto you
That one of your twelve   will become untrue,
One will sell Me   among the kinship of Jews,
Will sell Me for silver,   and will take such riches,
Such precious treasure;   and give his Lord in return,
His sweet, his beloved Liege.   But great sorrow shall come
                    unto him
From that deed, and much pain.   For he shall perceive them,
The Weird Sisters,   and shall see the end of his care.
He shall know most truly   that it would be a far sweeter
                    thing,
A far better one,   if he had never been born
To live in this light,   than that he take pay
For evil deeds   and wrongful advise."
Then each earl began   to look around at the others,
To gaze about sorrowfully,   for they were sore of soul
And troubled indeed of heart;   they heard their Lord there
Speaking words of lament.   They were worried
To which of the twelve   He would now tell
That he was the miscreant,   the man who had bargained
With the people for the pieces of silver.   Nor was it
                    simple for any person,
For any thane to confess   such a crime,
Such a sinful mind;   but each man denied it —
And all became fearful   and dared not ask
Until Simon Peter,   though he himself dared not speak —
This worthy man   did make motion
To John the good: to the Bairn of God
He was in these days   the dearest one,
The one most beloved,   and Holy Christ gave him leave
To rest in His lap,   to lie against His breast,
And on it to lean his head;   there heard he so many a
                    holy mystery,

So many deep thoughts; and to his dear Lord he did speak
And began to question Him. "Who shall that be, my Liege?"
Quoth he, "Who would sell Thee, the Richest of Kings,
To the folk of the foe? Full anxious we are,
O Wielder, to know." He had ready His words,
The Holy Christ: "See thou into whose hands I here
Give of My meat before these men: he hath most wicked
    thoughts,
Beareth great bitterness of mind: he shall deliver Me
    into bonds,
Into the power of the foe, where they shall deprive Me
    of My age,
Shall destroy My life." Thereafter He did take
The meat before the men and gave of the meat unto that
    mean scoundrel,
Into Judas' hand, and He spoke unto him,
He Himself before His disciples, and He straightway com-
    manded
That he fare far away from the folk. "Do as thou thinkest,"
    quoth He,
"Do as thou needst must do; no longer mayest thou
Hide thy will and intent — thy Weird is at hand,
Thy time draweth near." When the troth-breaker
Did take of the meat and with his mouth did eat thereof,
The power of God did forsake him, and the Fiend did enter
Into his body then, that loathsome wight;
And Satan was bound more sorely to him,
Bound hard 'round his heart, since the help of God
Had left him here in this light. To those who change lords
Under this heaven: to such woe will indeed come.

LVI

Then setting out from there and thinking up evil,
Judas did leave; against his Liege this thane
Harbored great grimness of heart. It had grown very dark,
It was deep in the night. Now the Son of the Lord

Tarried still at the feast;   and for His disciples there
The Wielder did bless   both the wine and the bread,
The Holy King of the Heavens;   and with His hands He did
                              break it
And gave it to His disciples   and gave thanks unto God,
Grateful unto Him,   who created all that was there,
The world and its winsomeness;   and He spoke many a word:
"Believe ye this clearly," quoth He,   "that this is My
                              body
And My blood as well.   I give both unto you
To eat and to drink.   This I shall give on earth,
Shall spill and spread onto it,   and shall ransom you
To the realms of the Lord   and to life everlasting
In the light of Heaven.   Remember ye ever
And follow ye that which I give   unto you at this feast.
Make it known unto the many,   for this is a mighty thing.
With it ye shall honor Him,   who is your Lord.
Hold this to My memory as a holy token,
So that the children of men   will cherish and keep it,
All men in this mid-world: that through My love I have
                              done so,
Through the grace of the Lord.   And think ye ever
How I have bidden you   to keep firm this brotherhood,
To have fastness of mind, much love in your hearts,   so
                    that the children of men
Over the whole of the earth   will all understand
That ye are most truly   the disciples Mine.
I shall also make known unto you   how a fierce, wily
                              Fiend,
A sword-strong foe   shall tempt your spirits,
Satan himself.   He cometh to ensnare
Your souls most boldly.   Straightway must ye make stead-
                              fast
The thoughts in your breasts.   By your prayers shall I
                              stand,
So that the mighty Fiend may not cause   your minds to
                    become doubtful,

So that I may help you against the foe.   Once he came
                    hither to tempt Me;
But his desire   sufficed not one whit,
His lust for My body.   Nor will I longer conceal from you
What trials now lie   straight ahead for you:
Ye shall be disloyal to Me,   ye disciples Mine,
Disloyal to your thaneship   before this dark night
Leaveth the land-folk   and the light cometh once more,
The morning to mankind."   Then the minds of the men
Became dreary,   their hearts sore indeed.
They were troubled of spirit,   and for their Lord's words
Most sorrowed and grieved.   But Simon Peter,
The thane, did speak   words of solace to the folk,
For love of his Lord.   "Though all this land-folk,"
                    quoth he,
"Though all Thy disciples deny Thee,   still do I gladly
Suffer all pain,   all sorrow for Thee.
I am ever prepared,   if God doth permit me,
To stand straight and firm   as a shield unto Thee.
Though they close Thee deep   in their dungeons,
Though the land-folk lock Thee away,   there is doubt so
                    little
But that I would bide   with Thee in Thy bonds,
Lie with Thee, my so beloved Lord,   if they lie in wait
To snuff out Thy life   with the hate of the sword's edge,
O my Master most Good;   then shall I gladly give up my
                    life
For Thee in the play of weapons,   nor verily shall I
Ever avoid it,   as long as mind
And strength of hand are still mine."   Then His Lord
                    spoke again unto him.
"Why, thou presumest in thyself," quoth He,   "an unswerving
                    loyalty.
A steadfastness so great!   Oh, thou hast the soul of a
                    hero
And good will as well.   Yet may I tell unto thee how
                    it will hap,

That thou shall'st become so wavering of heart,   as thou
                now canst not ween:
That thou shallst deny Me,   thy Lord, three times,
Before the crow of the cock,   acknowledging Me not as thy
                Liege,
But thou shallst renounce My protection."   Then again
                the man did reply.
"If in this world," quoth he,   "it will ever so come to
                pass,
That I should have to face   death together with Thee,
Have to die in splendor,   still that day will never arrive
When I would deny Thee,   my most dearly loved Lord,
Of my own will before these, the Jews."   All the disciples
                spoke likewise,
That they would suffer with Him   at the tribunal there.

LVII

Then the Wielder Himself   bade them with His words,
The High King of Heaven,   that they let not their hearts
                doubt,
Hight that they not want ...   deep thought[1]
"Let not your hearts be laid low   by the word of your Lord,
Nor fear ye too much.   I shall seek Our Father Myself
And shall send the Holy Ghost   from the kingdom of Heaven.
He shall be consolation   and succor both unto you,
Reminding you in His speech   of the many things I have
                taught
Unto you with My words.   Wisdom He will give unto you
In your hearts, a joyous teaching,   so that ye shall hence-
                forth accomplish
The word and the work   which I have shown unto you in this
                world."
The Mighty Son then rose,   Christ Savior,
In the temple there,   and with His thanes He fared forth,

[1] Lacuna in MS.

He Himself on that very same night.   Christ's disciples
Went sorrowing   and grieving most sadly,
Troubled of heart.   Then He climbed up a hill —
The Olive Mount was it called: there 'twas His custom
To go with His followers.   Full well did Judas know this,
The man with his mind aimed to ruin: for on this mount
                    he was often with Him.
Then God's Son did indeed   greet His disciples.
"Ye are now so saddened," quoth He,   "since ye know of
                    My death.
Now ye are grieving and groaning,   while the Jews are gay,
While the many are merry   and happy of mind,
While the world is in rapture.   Yet this will all come
                    to an end,
Will cease most swiftly.   Then will they be sore of heart,
Grow mournful of mind,   and ye may rejoice
Until that day everlasting;   for your end and a turn
Of your fortune never cometh: therefore may ye hence-
                    forth
Not regret My words nor rue My coming."   Then He bade
                    His retainers
Come on the mountain;   quoth that He wished them to climb
Higher up with Him   upon the hill-cliff,
And He hight that three   of His thanes go with Him,
Jacob and John   and Peter the Good,
Loyal thanes three.   And they did so go
With their Liege most gladly.   Then the Son of God,
Upon the hill, did bid them   bend their knees in prayer,
Bade that they greet God   and entreat Him greatly
That He hold in check   the strength of the Tempter
The will of the wicked,   so that the worker of wrong,
The devil, could not bring   their minds to doubt.
And also the Lord   Himself for prayer
Did bow with bent knee,   the Brightest of Kings,
Kneeling forward to earth;   and to the Father of all Earth-
                    folk
He cried aloud,   spoke lamenting words

162

In His sorrow;   for His spirit was grieved
And His heart was moved   by His humanness.
His flesh feared indeed;   tears fell from Him,
His dear, precious sweat did drip,   even as blood doth
                    drip,
Doth well from a wound.   Within God's Bairn
A battle was raging   between body and spirit.
The one was ready   for the road beyond,
The spirit for the kingdom of God,   while the other stood
                    yammering,
The flesh of Christ;   and fearful of death,
It sought not to give up the light.   Ever He cried to the
                    Lord,
Ever more did He call   unto the Almighty,
To the High Father of Heaven,   to the Holy God,
To the All-Wielder ever   with His words. "If mankind,"
                    quoth He,
"Cannot be saved   except that I give
My own precious blood   to the bairns of the people
To torture most terribly —   if this be truly Thy will,
Then will I choose to drain it: I take in my hands the
                    chalice,
Drink it down to the dregs,   my Lord, dear Liege,
Mighty Master and Shielder.   Look Thou not now down on
                    Me,
On the good of My flesh.   But I shall fulfill
Whatsoever Thy will be: for Thou wieldest power over all."
Then He went to that place,   where He had left His disciples
Biding upon the mountain;   and the Bairn of God
Did find them in troubled sleep;   for their hearts were
                    sore,
That they should be parted   from their beloved Liege.
Such should be the mind-sorrow   of every man
Who must forsake and leave   his beloved lord,
Giving up one so good.   Then He did go to His disciples,
                    spoke unto them;
The Wielder did wake them   and greet them with words.

"Why do ye wish to sleep?" quoth He.   "Why do ye not watch
But a little time here with Me?   That Weird is at hand,
That it shall so come to pass,   even as He, God the
                                        Father,
The Mighty, hath marked it.   There is no doubt in My mind;
My spirit is most ready   to make done God's will,
Is prepared to fare on His way.   But My flesh is still
                                        troubled,
My body still holds Me bound.   It is loathe to bear,
To endure such suffering.   But I shall accomplish
My Father's will.   Have ye firmness of heart!"
He did go then   up on the other side
Of the mountain   in order to pray —
The Glorious Lord —   and many a good word
He did indeed speak there.   God's angel then came
Holy from Heaven   and made firm His heart,
Made Him bold for the bonds.   He bided there ever,
Zealous in prayer,   and to His Father He cried,
To the Wielder with His words.   "If it cannot be other-
                                        wise," quoth He,
"O Lord most splendid,   except that I suffer
Great torture and torment for the folk   of mankind, I
                                        shall truly
Await then Thy will."   And He went again thence
To seek His disciples.   He found them sleeping
And called to them curtly.   And again He went thence
A third time to pray.   And the King of All Peoples,
The Son of the Lord, spoke   with the selfsame words
To His All-Wielding Father,   as He had done before.
Most zealously   did Savior Christ
Remind the Mighty One   of the good of mankind;
And went then again to His disciples,   and straightway He
                                        spoke unto them.
"Sleep ye and rest," said He.   "Now will he straightway come,
Come with a force, he who hath sold Me,   sinless as I am,
And hath received silver therefore."   The disciples of
                                        Christ

Awakened after these words,   and they beheld war-men coming,
Climbing up the mountain   with a great commotion,
Wrathful weapon-bearers full many.

LVIII

Judas rightly did lead them,
Man hate-filled of heart.   After him the Jews did go
                              marching,
The folk-clans of the foe.   In their midst they carried
                              fire,
Lights in lamp-vessels;   and they led forth torches,
Bright burning down from the city,   as they began most
                              eagerly
To stride up the mountain.   This spot Judas knew well,
The one to which he should lead   the land-folk all.
As they now fared to the spot   in front of the folk,
He said unto them as a sign,   lest they seize by mistake
Some other man: "I shall first go to Him," quoth he,
"Shall kiss Him and say: that is Christ Himself!
Then shall ye seize Him   with the strength of the crowd;
Shall bind Him up there on the mount   and bring Him down
                              to the bastion,
Lead Him down 'mid the land-folk: His life hath he for-
                              feited
With His words full well."   And the people went,
Until they were come   to the Christ Himself —
The grim folk of the Jews,   to where He stood with His
                              followers,
The Lord Most Glorious,   biding his god-sent fate,
The wonderous time.   Then Judas went toward Him,
Man without troth,   and unto God's Bairn
He nodded His head   and here spoke to his Lord,
Kissed Him, Mighty Christ,   carried out his word,
Pointed Him out to the people,   as he had promised before.
The Lord of All Peoples   bore all with His patience,
The Wielder of World;   and with His words He did speak
                              unto him,

Asked him most boldly: "Why hast thou come to Me with this
                                 host?
Why dost thou lead this land-folk to Me?   And to this
                           loathsome crowd
Thou sellest Me with thy kiss,   among the clans of the Jews
Betrayest Me to these many?"   He went to speak to the many,
To the other people,   and to ask with His words
Why they were come to seek Him   so zealouly here
With their thralls in the night.   "To whom do you wish to
                           bring need and distress,
To some one of mankind.?"   Then once more the many did speak
                           unto Him
And said that they had been told   that the Savior did tarry
Here high on the hillside.   "He who hath caused this unrest
Amid the Jewish folk   and calleth Himself
The Son of God.   We came here to seek Him,
Are most anxious to find Him: He is from Galilee-land
From the city of Nazareth."   When Saving Christ
Said unto them in sooth   that it was He Himself,
The folk of the Jews   became sore afraid.
Frightened and shocked were they,   so that they straight-
                           way fell back,
Each and all, and sought the earth: at the same time
All the host did retreat.   They could not resist
The word and the voice of the Lord;   yet were there some
                           warlike men.
These ran up the hillock;   made firm their hearts,
Bound fast the thoughts in their breasts;   and bitterly
                           raging,
They surrounded Christ Savior.   There stood the wise men
Grieving greatly —   Christ's goodly disciples,
Before this most dreadful deed;   and to their Dear Lord they
                           did speak:
"Were it now Thy will," quoth they,   "My Wielder, My Liege,
That they shall slay us   with the spear-point here,
Shall wound us with weapons,   then would nought be one
                           whit as good,

166

But that we might die   here for our Dear Lord,
Pale in expiring.   Then plenteously wroth grew he,
The swift swordsman,   Simon Peter.
It welled up with his heart,   so that not a word could he
                        speak,
So sorrowed his soul,   since they were about to enchain
His Beloved Lord there.   Bloated with anger, the bold-minded
Thane strode ahead,   stood before his Liege,
Hard by his Lord;   nor was his heart e'er in doubt,
Fearful within his breast,   but he drew his bill,
The sword at his side,   and with the strength of his arm
He struck the first of the foe   standing before him,
So that Malchus   was marked by the knife
On his right side,   slashed by the sword's edge.
His hearing had been hewn: sore was the hurt 'round his
                        head,
So that sword-gory,   cheek and ear in mortal wound
Burst asunder,   and blood did spring forth,
Welling up from the wound.   Then was the cheek indeed scarred
Of the enemy's leader.   Those around stood away,
Dreading the bite of the bill.   Then spake God's Bairn
Himself to Simon Peter, said   that he should put his sword,
The sharp one, back in its scabbard.   "If I truly cared,"
                        said He
"To wage conflict   against this crowd of the warriors,
Then would I remind Him, the Glorious,   the Almighty God,
The Holy Father   in the Kingdom of Heaven,
That He send hither to Me   a host of His angels,
Wise in warfaring;   these men could indeed not withstand
Their weapon-strength ever.   Nor could such a host of
                        warriors
Stand against them, though gathered   together in groups.
Still could they not save their lives.   But the All-
                Wielding Lord,
The Father Almighty,   hath marked it otherwise:
We are to bear all the bitterness,   whatsoever these
                people bring unto us,

Nor shall we be angry   nor rage 'gainst their strife:
For he who doth practice   the hatred of weapons,
Who gladly partaketh   in grim spear-grudges —
He again is slain   by the sword's edge,
Doth die in his own blood.   We must not destroy
One whit with our deeds."   Then He went to the wounded man.
With skill He set   the flesh-seams together,
The head-wounds all,   so that it was healed straightway,
The bite of the bill.   And the Bairn of God
Spake to the angry throng.   "Methinks 'tis a wonder great,"
                quoth He,
"If ye have wanted   to do harm unto Me,
Why did ye then not take Me,   when I stood in the temple,
Among your folk and did tell them   full many true words?
The sun shone, the day's dear beam,   and ye did want to do
Naught to harm there in this light;   but now ye lead your
                landsmen
To Me in the night,   as one doeth unto a thief
Whom one wishes to seize —   some scoundrel and wretch
Who hath forfeited life."   Then the folk of the Jews
Grasped at God's Son,   the grim-minded host,
The persecuting crowd.   The people piled 'round Him,
The enraged horde of men —   they saw not their wrongs —
They held Him fast,   threw His hands in chains,
His arms and fingers in fetters.   Such frightful torment
He needed not have stood,   nor such grievous suffering,
Nor have endured such anguish.   But He did so for this
                host,
Since He wanted to save   the children of men,
To fetch them from hell   to the kingdom of Heaven,
To the wide-flung wealth;   therefore He reproached them no
                whit
For that which they would do unto Him   in their hatred and
                anger.

LIX

Then the angry folk of the Jews   did become insolent,
The host most haughty,   since they had Holy Christ
And could lead Him away   in limb-bondage,
Take Him forth in their fetters.   And the foe went again
From the mount to the town.   And God's Mighty Bairn
Did go 'mid the host   with His hands all bound,
Drear and sad, down to the dale.   For His dearest thanes
Had broken their troth,   as He Himself had foretold.
But it was not for fear   that they forsook Him,
God's Bairn, their Beloved,   but so long before there had
           been
The word of the prophet,   that it would indeed be thus.
Therefore they could not avoid their own deeds.   And after
           the crowd
Went Peter and John,   those two men well-known,
And followed from afar.   Full anxious were they
To know what the grim-minded Jews   meant to do with God's
           Bairn,
To their Lord most Dear.   When they were come down to the
           dale
From the hill to the burg   in which was their bishop,
The temple's holder,   these haughty men did lead Him
These earls, behind a fence.   A great fire was there,
There were flames in the foreyard,   made nearby for the
           folk,
For the warrior crowd.   They went there to warm them,
The landsmen of Jews,   and they left God's Bairn
Waiting in chains.   There was a great racket,
The noise of the insolent.   Since John was known
To the highest one there,   he could push inside with the
           host,
With the throng through the yard;   but the best of all thanes,
Peter, still stood outside.   The portal's warder would not
           permit him
To follow His Lord,   till he begged a friend,

Until John begged of   a Jew to let Peter go
Forth to the foreyard.   A woman full of deceit
Did slip up to him there: she was a handmaid
Of one of the Jews, of her lord;   and this unlovely girl
Did speak to the thane.   "What, thou mightest be," quoth
                    she, "a man
From Galilee, disciple   of Him standing yonder
With His arms firmly fettered."   Then fear overtook
Simon Peter straightway,   and his mind became slack,
And he said that not one word   of the wife had he understood,
Nor was He a thane of that Leader   ever, of that Lord.
He avoided Him in view of the many,   said verily he knew
                    not that Man.
"Thy talk is senseless to me," said he.   Then God's strength,
The Lord's power did leave his heart.   And leaving, he did
                    go
Forth amid the folk,   until he came to the fires;
He went there to warm him.   There also a woman began
To load loathsome words unto him.   "Here may ye look on
                    your foe," cried she,
"This is all clearly   a retainer of Christ,
A disciple of Him Himself."   Then straightway there did
                    come nearer
To him men of the foe.   And the bairns of the Fiend
Did question him   of what clan he was:
"Thou art not of these burghers,"   quoth they. "From thy
                    bearing we see that,
From thy words and thy ways,   that thou art not of this
                    world-folk,
But art from Galilee come."   Yet he would not admit it,
But stood there denying   and swore a strong oath
By all that is true   that he was not of that tribe.
His words had no power: it was to come to this pass,
As He who rules mankind   had so marked it indeed
In this world. Then came   to him also a cousin
Of him whom he   had hewn with his bill,
With his sword's sharpness;   and said that he had seen
                    him there

"High on the hillock,   there where we bound the hands
Of thy Lord in the grove,   in the tree-garden there,
Fastened His arms with the fetters."   Then for the fear
                    in his heart
He again denied his dear Liege,   quoth that indeed he would
                    forfeit his life,
If there was any man   here on this earth
Who can say in truth   that he was of that tribe,
That he followed His path.   There for the first time
The crow of the cock did commence.   And Holy Christ,
The Best of All Bairns,   who stood there bound,
The Son of the Lord Himself,   did look to Simon Peter,
Saw that earl over His shoulder.   Then Simon Peter
Felt sadness within him   and his spirit was sore.
Filled with hurt was his heart,   and most grieved was he.
So troubled was he,   that he himself had so spoken before,
And he remembered the words then   which All-Wielding
                    Christ
Had said unto him;   that in this swarthy, dark night,
He was to deny Him,   his Lord, three times,
Before the crow of the cock.   Bitterly this came up in
                    his breast,
Welled up with him;   and angry of heart he went away:
The man left the many.   With care in his mind
And deeply sorrowed,   he wept at his sinfulness,
At his own words,   and there came welling up
Hot tears from within him   for the grief in his heart,
Bloodily bursting up   from his breast. For he thought
Never to atone for his sins   nor come again to his Master,
To the grace of his Lord.   No one hath since grown so old
Who ever did see   a man rue more sorely
His own words and his sins   and to bewail them so,
Lamenting most loudly.   "Woe, Mighty God, O my Lord," quoth
                    he,
"Woe that I have forfeited myself,   so that for this world,
This life I may no longer be thankful.   If in my old age
I must renounce Thy grace   and the realms of Heaven,

Then my Ruler, my King,   be there no thanks unto me,
My Beloved Liege,   that I was born to this light.
I am now unworthy,   O Thou, my Wielder,
That I may thus fare   along with Thy followers,
Sinful amid Thy disciples.   I myself shall avoid them
In my heart and my soul,   since I have spoken such sin."
Thus the best of all men   grieved bitterly indeed.
He rued most deeply   that he had denied Him there,
His Beloved Lord.   But the bairns of the land-folk,
Of mankind should not wonder   why God so willed it,
That such a beloved man   should suffer such sorrow,
That he should deny   his Lord so disgracefully
For the word of a servant maid —   he, this swiftest of
                                                            warriors
Deny his Dear Liege;   it was done for all those of mankind,
For the good of the children of men.   He wanted to make
                                                            them the first,
The highest over His household — He the Lord Holy:
He let it be known   how little strength hath
The heart of man   without God's might.
He let him sin   so that later he might
Better believe them, the people,   how precious it is
For each man indeed,   when he hath done evil,
That he be absolved   from his wicked deeds,
From his wrongs and his sins,   as he is absolved by God
                                                            Himself,
The Ruler of Heaven's Realms,   from his hurtful wrong.

LX

Therefore is a man's boasting   of but little avail —
The pride of his youth: if then God's help doth forsake
                                                            him,
Because of his sins,   then is that man straightway
Fearful of thought,   though he first uttered threats
And boasted of his battles   and of the broad strength of
                                                            his hand —

This man of his might.   This was marked in that marvelous,
That best of all thanes,   when at that time the holy help
Of His Master forsook him.   Therefore no man should boast
All too much of himself,   since then often hope
And will do forsake him,   if All-Wielding God,
The High King of Heaven,   doth not strengthen his heart.
But the Best of All Bairns did wait   and did bear His
                              bonds
For the sake of mankind.   Many of the Jewish folk
Did come and surround Him   and speak such mockery
And held Him to scorn,   as He stood there chained
And enduring most patiently   what the people did unto Him,
What loathsome grief these land-folk.   Then was the light
                              come again,
The morning to mankind.   Many were gathered,
Wide hosts of the Jews.   Wolf-minds had they,
Evil hearts as well.   Their book-learned ones,
Many men together,   gathered at morning-tide,
Angry and hardened   and longing for evil,
Wishing for wrong.   They went in groups together,
The men to consult;   and they began to consider
How they would accuse   the Mighty Christ of sin
With false witnesses   and with faithless men —
Accuse Him indeed   through His own spoken word,
So that they might torment Him   with tortures most great,
Dealing out death unto Him.   But on that day they could
Find no false witnesses,   ones who feared not
To deal out such pain,   and to condemn Him to death,
Release Him from life.   Then at last there came forth
From the crowd two men without truth   and began to tell
                              against Him,
Said that they had heard Him   Himself say
That He could tear down   the temple of God,
The highest of all houses,   through the strength of His
                              hands;
And through His craft and His might   could erect it again
On the third day hence,   as no other man could ever thus
                              do.

He was silent and suffered.   Never could a folk speak,
A people utter such lies,   that He would verily
Have avenged them with words of evil.   Then there arose
                    from the host
A man baleful of thought: bishop among the folk,
A prince of this people — and put such question to
                    Christ,
Exhorted Him strongly   with solemn oath,
Greeted Him thus in the name of God   and bade Him eagerly
To say unto him,   whether He were the Son
Of the Living God: He who created the light,
Christ, King Eternal.   "We cannot see one whit of this
From Thy words or Thy works."   Then verily again the
                    True,
The Good Son of God did reply: "Thou sayest it now before
                    these Jews,
Sayest it truly,   that it is I Myself.
But these landsmen do not believe Me;   and hence will they
                    not release Me,
Nor are they worthy of My word.   Now verily I say unto
                    you
That ye shall still see Me   sitting on the right side
                    of God,
Radiant the Son of Man   in the might and strength
Of the All-Wielding Father,   and coming again down here
Through the clouds of Heaven   and dealing unto all the
                    kith of mankind
Such judgments with His words,   even as they worked and
                    are worthy thereof."
Then was the bishop wrathful   and bitter of heart,
Sorely enraged at these words;   and he rent his raiments,
Tore them before his breast;   "Now need ye bide no longer,"
                    quoth he,
"Ye people, wait for a witness,   now that such words,
Such blasphemy hath come from His mouth.   Many men have now
                    heard it:
Warriors here in the temple,   that He told of His mightiness,

Said that He was the God.   Well then, ye Jews,
What doom will ye deal Him?   Is He now worthy of death
For such words?"

LXI

The war-men all spoke,
The folk of the Jews,   that He had forfeited life,
Was worthy of punishment.   Yet not for His works was it
                    done,
That the Jewish folk   there in Jerusalem
Condemned Him to His death,   Him who had done no sin,
The Son of the Lord.   Then the land-folk of Jews
Did boast of their deeds,   how they could do God's Bairn,
Him held in bonds,   the most harm indeed.
The crowd surrounded Him   and struck His cheeks, the side
Of His head with their hands: unto Him they did this in
                    mockery and scorn,
The crowd of the foe;   covered Him with their malice
And their blasphemous speech.   And the Bairn of God
Stood firmly amid His foe.   His arms were in fetters;
He endured most patiently   what the people
Brought unto Him of bitterness there.   He bore no anger
Against this riot of men.   Then wrathful men
Did take Him so bound,   that Bairn of God,
And they led Him there   to where the folk-throng's
The people's judging-place was.   There thanes aplenty
Surrounded their leader.   He was the envoy of that lord
Of the city of Rome,   who ruled over all realms;
He was come from Caesar, was sent to the clans of the Jews,
To govern their kingdom: he gave them counsel.
Pilate was he called,   and he was a man from Pontus,
Born of that clan.   He had collected a great crowd,
A multitude of the people   at the judging place.
This faithless horde   of the Jewish host
Did give Him up —   Him, Son of God,
To the folk of the foe;   quoth that He had forfeited His
                    life

And that one should reward Him   with the weapon's edge,
With the sword's sharpness.   Still the crowd of the Jews
                              cared not
To throng into the law-house itself;   but the land-folk
                              did remain without,
And spoke from there to the many within.   Into this mob
                              they wished not to go,
Not go to that foreign man,   so that they need not hear
                              these unrighteous words
On that day, nor hear one whit   of the wrong being dealt.
But said it was their wont to hold   the holiest of times,
The purest, their Passover.   Pilate received
The Wielder's Bairn   from the wicked sinners,
Received Him, the Sinless.   Then sorely troubled
Was Judas of mind,   when he saw His Master
Surrounded to death;   and his deed he now began
To rue in his heart,   that he had sold Him,
His Lord without Sin.   He took the silver,
Took there the thirty pieces   that they had given to him
                              in return for his Liege.
And he went with them to the Jews   and told them his grim,
                              wicked deed,
Said unto them his sin;   and the silver he offered
To give back gladly.   "So grievously," quoth he,
"Have I sold it, the blood   of my Liege, my Beloved,
That I ween that to me   it will be of no worth."
But the host of the Jews would not take it,   but hight
                              him henceforth
To let such a sin   be his own care and concern,
That e'er he had done   against his Lord.
"Thou thyself look to that," quoth they.   "What hast thou
                              to seek among us?
Do not thou place shame on these people."   Then presently
                              Judas
Did again go thence   to the temple of God
Most sorely grieved,   and he threw the silver
Inside on the altar,   nor dared he own it for long.

He fared forth in fear   and the bairns of the Fiend
Admonished him fiercely: the devil had seized
The mind of this man;   and the Mighty God was enraged,
So that he, that wretch,   did fashion a rope;
And in order to hang him,   did incline his head
Through the death-choking noose,   and chose his reward,
The hard pangs of hell,   those hot and most dark,
The deep dale of death;   since unto his Liege he had in-
                deed been disloyal.

LXII

Suffering His bonds,   God's Bairn still did bide,
Did wait at the law-house   until the land-folk
About Him became   all of one mind
As to what terrible torture   they intended for Him.
Then the envoy of Caesar   arose from the bench —
He, come from Rome;   and he went to speak angrily
To the crowd of the Jews,   there where in the courtyard
The many were milling about.   The multitude would not come
Into the house on the Paschal day.   Pilate began
To question boldly   about the folk of the Jews,
Why this Man indeed   did deserve His murder,
Had reaped such punishment.   "Why now are ye wroth,
So hostile of mind to this Man?"   They said that He had
                harmed them muchly,
Had done them great wrong.   "The folk would not give Him
                over to thee,
If they knew not already   that noxious He was and evil:
He hath forfeited His life with His words.   Full many a
                one of the folk
Hath He seduced with His teachings,   hath distressed these
                people,
Caused their minds to doubt: that to Caesar's court
We need pay no tithe.   That may we tell of Him
With truthful witness.   Great words speaketh He also:
Doth say He is the Christ,   King over that realm.

With His bigness is He bloated." But then Caesar's envoy
Did speak again unto them. "If He hath so openly
Done deeds of evil," quoth he, "among the multitude,
Then take Him back among your folk; and if He hath for-
feited His life,
Deal ye His doom, if He is deserving of death,
As your age-old laws do order you."
Still at this time on this hallowed day,
Quoth they, they could not kill with their weapons,
Become murderers of any man whatsoever.
Then he turned away from the horde — that man, evil-
hearted,
The thane of Caesar, who was over his throngs,
The envoy from Rome — and he ordered right quickly
That the Bairn of God be brought closer to him; and
bluntly
And carefully questioned Him, whether He was King of this
crowd,
Of this land-folk here. And the Son of the Lord
Had ready His word, asking "Whether thou speakest that
for thyself,
Or whether for others, the earls here, have
Told of My kingdom?" Then truly the envoy of Caesar
Spoke again, evil and insolent of mind, as he wrangled
With Christ Wielder there in the temple. "I am not,"
quoth he,
"Of this kingdom, of the Jews, am no kin of Thine,
No kith of these men, but the many have consigned Thee
to me,
Thy landsmen, the folk of the Jews have given Thee fettered
Into my hands. What harm hast Thou done,
That so bitterly Thou must suffer Thy bondage?
Torture from Thy own true kin?" Then Christ did tell him
again,
The Best of All Saviors, as He stood there bound
Inside the temple. "My kingdom," quoth He, "is not
Of this hour, of this earthly life. If it were thus,

My disciples would be standing   strong against the strife-
                minded,
My followers, thanes   resisting the throng.
Nor fettered, would I   be given o'er to the folk
Of the hating, the Jews,   into their hands
To be tortured most terribly.   Truly was I born to this
                world
To make known unto you   a testimony of truth
Through My coming.   And that they well may acknowledge,
Those men who have strayed from the truth: they may hear
                My word,
Understand and believe My lesson."   Then the envoy of
                Caesar
Could not find a whit   of fault with God's Bairn,
Not a word of deceit   for which He was worthy
Of paying His life.   Then he repaired   once more to the
                people of Jews
To speak with them angrily.   And he said to the many
Who hearkened most carefully,   that he could find
No such blasphemous speech,   that He should pay with His
                life,
Be worthy of death.   Then dull-minded,
The Jewish folk did stand   and accused God's Son
With their words and said that He had first   stirred in-
                surrection
And unrest in Galilee-land;   and from there had repaired
Hither over Judea;   and He caused hearts to doubt,
The minds of men,   "and for that He deserves to be murdered,
Is worthy of death   with the weapons's edge,
If ever a man was deserving   of death for such deeds."

LXIII

The landsmen of Jews lamented   loudly to him with their
                words,
Their hearts all hate-filled;   then the high lord,
The sly-minded man,   heard them say unto him

From which of the clanships   Christ had been born,
The Best of All Men: He belonged to a glorious band
From Galilee-land — Christ the Good.   There dwelt a great
                    crowd,
A host of aethling-born men.   Herod held there
A strong, goodly kingdom,   which Caesar had given unto him,
The mighty from Rome;   and there he dealt justice,
Practiced right 'mid the people,   keeping the peace
And dealing out dooms.   On that day also
He was there in Jerusalem   with his thanes and retainers
And came to the temple: that was their custom
That they held sacred   the holy tide
The Passover of Jews.   Pilate then bade
That the soldiers take   that Man in His chains,
Take Him in His bonds,   the Bairn of God,
Hight that the earls   bring Him to Herod,
His hands held in fetters,   since He was of that folk
Over which Herod wielded power.   The warriors accomplished
The word of their lord.   They led Holy Christ
Forth in His fetters   in front of the folk-leader.
The Best of All Bairns   who had ever been born
To the light of the land-folk.   In His limb-bonds he went,
Until they did bring Him   there where he sat on his bench —
Herod the king.   A crowd of people surrounded him,
Proud-minded warriors;   a great will was within them
To see Christ Himself,   for they weened He would show
                    them
Some token, as indeed   He had done through His godliness
Before the crowd of the Jews: He, Christ Great and Mighty;
Then the folk-king did question Him —   full envious was
                    he,
Asked many a word   and wanted to fathom
How His spirit inclined,   what He minded to do
For the weal of men.   There stood Mighty Christ,
Was silent and suffered.   He chose not to answer him,
Herod, the folk-king,   nor the earls of his following,
Not with one single word.   Then the wicked throng,

The folk of the Jews stood there,   and the Son of God.
They did worry and accuse Him wildly,   until the world-
                         king
Became enraged of heart,   and his retainers as well:
In their spirits they scorned Him;   for they saw the great
                         might of God,
Of the Lord of all Heaven;   and in their heart there was
                         darkness
In the grip of sin.   But the Son of the Lord
Endured their direful works,   their words and their deeds,
Suffered them all   with a humble soul,
All the wrongs they longed   to do unto Him.
They ordered white robes   wrapped around Him, 'round His
                         limbs
In mockery; all the more   He became for the men there,
For the young ones, a jest;   and the Jews did rejoice,
When they saw how those   held Him in scorn,
Those earls overweening.   Then Herod again,
The king, sent Him thence   to the other clanships.
He hight that a strong man   should lead Him hence; and
                         they spoke
To Him sinfully, heaped blasphemy   on Him as He went in
                         His bonds,
And they laughed in mockery.   But His mind never doubted,
But He suffered all   with a humble spirit;
He wished not to repay them   for their wicked words,
For their mocking speech and their scorn.   They brought
                    Him inside the house,
Up in the palace,   where Pilate was
In the judging place there.   The thralls then did give
The Best of All Bairns   into the hands of the baleful,
The murderers — Him without sin,   as He Himself chose.
He wanted to free the bairns of mankind   from the bonds
                         of death,
To save them from suffering.   The foe stood around,
Jews before the guest halls: the bairns of the devil
Had stirred up the horde,   so that they did not hold back

From these grim, wicked deeds.   Then he went forth,
The thane of Caesar,   and to the folk he did speak,
The harsh leader of hosts.   "What, ye have sent Him here to
                                    the hall,
Sent this Man unto me in His bonds,   have yourselves blamed
                                    Him,
That He hath brought ruin   to right many folk,
With His lesson hath led them all wrongly.   Now from these
                                    landsmen,
From this folk, I cannot find   that He hath forfeited
His life, is guilty of aught.   That was indeed all clear
                        this day:
Herod, who knoweth your laws,   your people, your landways,
Could not in anger   end His life on this day,
Would not say He should die   for any sin of His —
Should take leave of this life.   Now before this land-folk
Shall I threaten Him with the law,   shall urge Him with words,
Shall better the thought   in His breast, so that henceforth
He may enjoy life among man."   But the multitude
Of Jews cried together,   called with loud voices
And eagerly hight   that He be robbed of His life —
Christ killed with torture   and struck on the cross,
Tormented to death.   "With His words He hath done it,
Hath forfeited life!   He sayeth He is the Lord,
Truly God's Son.   He shall now pay
For His evil speech;   so our law is indeed writ:
That one buyeth with one's life   such blasphemous speech."

LXIV

Then he who held sway o'er the folk   became sore afraid,
In his mind did fear mightily,   when he heard the men say
That they had heard Him   speak thus themselves,
Proclaiming in front of the clanships   that He was God's
                                    Son.
Then the leader of hosts   went back in the house,
Into the judging hall   and hailed God's Son

With confident words and questioned   what He was 'mid the
                              clans:
"What kind of man art Thou?" quoth he.   "Why concealest
                         Thou Thy mind,
Hidest Thy deepest thoughts?   Wist Thou that Thy life's
                              destiny
Standeth so, even as I   shall decide. Unto me have these
                              folk,
These people of Jews given Thee   to wield such power o'er
                              Thee,
Either to slay Thee   with the point of the spear,
To torture Thee unto the cross,   or to leave Thee quick
                         and alive,
Even as I myself   deem it better
To act for my people."   Then the Peace-Bairn of God spoke
                         again:
"Thou wist most verily,"   quoth He, "that thou would'st wield,
Wouldst have no might over Me,   but that Holy God Himself
Hath granted it unto thee.   And those, too, have sinned more,
Those who have sent Me   to thee in their hatred,
Have sold Me, bound fast in these snares."   There straight-
                         way thereafter
The grim-souled man   would gladly have released Him,
The thane of the emperor   in front of the throng, if he could
                         have but done so.
But they denied him his will   with their every word —
The clan-folk of Jews.   "Thou art not," quoth they, "Caesar's
                              friend,
The beloved of thy lord,   if thou leavest Him
To go hence sound and unharmed.   That may still bring thee
                              sorrow
And reprisal, too,   if a one speaketh such words,
Raiseth himself so high,   and sayeth that he here holdeth
The name of a kingdom,   though Caesar ne'er gave it,
He confuseth his world-realms   and bringeth scorn to his
                              word,
Mocking him in his mind.   Therefore must thou avenge such
                              wrongs,

These insolent words,   if thou hast worry for thy master's,
For thy liege-lord's friendship.   Then should'st thou reft
                         Him of life."
The duke now heard,   how the aethlings of the Jews
Threatened him with his liege;   therefore he went himself
And sat at the judging place,   where a great host of people
Was gathered together,   and hight Christ the Wielder
Be brought there in front of the folk.   The Jews then de-
                         manded
To see the Holy Bairn   first hanging in torment
There on the cross;   quoth that no other king
Would they have to oversee them,   except for high Caesar
From the city of Rome.   "He hath here his rule over us.
Therefore shalt thou not release Him;   He hath spoken
                    much harm unto us,
Hath done in His life through His deeds.   Death shall He
                    suffer here,
Punishment and the pangs of torture."   The people of Jews
Accused Mighty Christ   of so many,
Of such varied sins.   He stood silent
There in His humbleness,   and not a thing did He answer
To the wicked words.   He wanted to ransom
All men with His life.   Therefore He let the loathsome
                         mob
Torment Him most terribly,   as was truly His will.
Yet He had no wish   to reveal all things openly
To the people of Jews: that He Himself was indeed God.
For if they verily knew   that He wielded such might
Over the mid-world here,   then their minds would grow
                         fearful,
Be afraid in their breasts;   then God's Bairn they'd not
                         dare
To touch with their hands;   and the kingdom of Heaven,
The greatest of lights,   would never be unlocked to the
                    bairns of mankind.
Therefore He hid it well in His mind   and let not the
                    children of men

Know what they were working.   Then Weird came nearer,
God's glorious might,   and that great midday
When they would cause to be done   those death-torments.
There lay also in bonds   within the bastion
A notorious robber: in the realm he had
Committed murders aplenty   and done manslaughter.
He was known as a mighty thief.   Nor was there his like
                    anywhere.
He was in chains   because of his sins.
Barrabas was he hight,   and here in the burg
This man was far known   for his many misdeeds.
That was the land-custom   of the kinfolk of Jews
That each year for God's love   they could ask amnesty
On that holy day   for some man doomed to die;
And that the leader, warder of bastions,   would give him
                    his life.
Then the duke began   to question the gathering,
The folk of the Jews   who stood there before him
Which of the two   they wanted to have freed,
To beg for his life: "which are in bonds here,
In fetters in front of the clanships."   Then the folk of
                    the Jews
Had stirred up all   the poorer, the smaller men,
So that they asked for the life   of the land-robber:
They demanded the thief,   who in darkness of night
Had committed his crimes;   and All-Wielding Christ
They tortured onto the cross.   Then it became truly known
                    unto all
How the people had dealt out their dooms.   Then had they
                    to accomplish this deed
And to hang Him, the Holy Bairn.   In times hence that
                    would bring
To the duke great trouble,   when he truly knew
That the folk of the Jews   loathed Christ Savior as their
                    foe,
That they hated Him;   and that he, Pilate, had hearkened
                    unto them

And had granted their will;   for this he had evil reward,
Punishment here in this light   and for long ages after.
He won great woe,   when he later gave up this world.

LXV

The Wrong-Doer soon grew aware of this,   the greatest of
scoundrels,
Satan himself,   when the soul of Judas
Came down to the ground   of grim, hot hell.
Then most verily he knew   that it was All-Wielding Christ,
The Bairn of the Lord,   who stood there bound;
And most verily he knew   that He wished to release
The whole world and its people   from the pangs of hell
Through His hanging, leading them all   to the light of
the Lord.
Then was Satan   indeed sore of heart,
Most troubled of mind;   truly he hoped
To bring it about   that the bairns of mankind
Would not rob Christ of life,   nor torture Him on the
cross.
But he wanted Christ   to remain quick and alive,
So that the children of men   would not be safe from hell,
Safe from their sins.   Satan hied himself hence
To where was the house   of the host's leader
Within the bastions.   To the bride here openly,
To the wife within   the weird Fiend began
To reveal great wonders,   so that with her word-help
She would cause it to be   that Christ, Lord of Men,
Could remain 'mid the quick —   for already He was destined
to die —
For he knew most truly   that He would take from him the
power
So that he would no longer own so much   in this mid-world
here,
O'er this wide, wide earth.   The wife became fearful.
Sorely troubled was she,   since these visions did come
unto her

186

In the full light of day   through the doing of him
Who was hidden by a helmet of magic   to make him unseen.
With words did she plead with her husband: the wife did
                        hight
He be told most truly   what visions had come unto her
From the Holy Man;   and she bade him for help
To save His life.   "I have seen here so much through Him,
So many strange things,   that well do I know that the sins
Shall thrive indeed   of any aethling
Who so recklessly hopes   to rob Him of life."
The messenger went on his way,   until he did find the
                        folk-warden,
The duke sitting there   among the throng of the people
On the stony way,   there where the street
Is fused together with rocks.   And he fared to his lord
And told the word of the wife   unto him. And the folk-
                        warden
Became troubled of soul,   and he went inside.
The thoughts in his breast grew fearful,   for both were
                        grievous for him:
That they should slay Him,   who was free of sin,
And that before this crowd he dared not   leave that task
                        undone
Because of the people's word.   But then it was turned,
The heart in his breast,   as the host of the Jews did so
                        want it
To work their will.   He warded from himself
Not a single, dire sin,   which he himself there did.
He hight them bring him   a clear fount for his hands,
Bring him water in a vessel,   as he verily sat in front of
                        the folk
And the thane of Caesar   washed himself 'fore the throng,
The harsh leader of hosts,   and to the horde he did speak,
Said that he was freeing himself   from such sinful deeds,
Such wrongful works;   "Nor will I be responsible," quoth
                        he,
"Even one whit for this Holy Man;   but ye alone shall
                        carry out all

With your words and your works — all which ye do Him here
                    to His woe."
Then all the clanships of Jews cried out together,
The mighty multitude; quoth that against this man
They would carry out sentence for His evil deeds. "Let
                 His gore drip down —
His blood over us, and the bane of death — and over our
                 bairns as well —
O'er our children's children coming thereafter — we shall
                 still be responsible
For the slaying itself — supposing we commit thereby a
                 sin!"
There before the throng of the Jews the Best of All Men
                 was then given
Into the hand of the haters, held tightly by chains,
Forced into fetters — so the foe did receive Him —
Those who did loathe Him: the land-folk encircled Him,
The churls evil-minded. The Mighty Lord
Suffered patiently all that the people did unto Him.
They hight He be flogged before they would rob Him
Of His life, of His age; and under His eyes they spat at
                 Him.
They held Him up to their scorn, and with their hands
                 they did strike Him,
The men, 'gainst His cheeks, and of His garments they
                 stripped Him,
And then renegades robbed Him and took His red robe,
And gave Him another — ungracious were they —
And a wonderous headband, a crown of hard thorns
They hight wound round, and hight it be set on All-
                 Wielding Christ,
On Him there, Himself. And the thralls went to Him,
In kingly way did address Him, and fell on their knees,
And bowed their heads unto Him: in mockery of Him they
                 so did.
But all patiently He bore it, the Lord of the Peoples,
The Mighty One, for His love for the children of men.

Then they hight that the men work   with the weapon's edge,
Make with their hands   out of the hard wood
A great, strong cross,   and they hight that Christ,
God's Blessed Bairn   be brought there Himself;
Hight that they lead Him,   our Lord, where He was to
                              bleed
And to die — He without sin.   And the Jews all went,
The world-men, all willingly   and led All-Wielding Christ,
The Dear Lord to His death.   Dire things one could hear,
Grievous and wrong; groaning,   the women did go,
Did follow with weeping,   and the men were wailing,
Those come from Galilee,   who did go with them,
Faring from far-off ways.   For the death of their Fair Lord
They were sorrowing sorely.   But He Himself, looking back,
                              did see them,
Hight that they weep not,   "Nor may ye sorrow one whit
For My wayfaring hence,   but your wicked words
Ye may bewail   and lament with your weeping,
With your bitter tears.   For the time will come
When the mothers will rejoice,   the maids of Judea, that
                              in their lives
No bairn was e'er born unto them.   For then will ye bitter-
                              ly pay
For your wrongs, right grimly.   Then would ye be glad
If the high mountains   did hide you down here,
And bury you deeply.   Death would be dearer,
Lovelier for all in the land,   than to suffer the loath-
                              some
Murder of mankind,   which will come here to the kinships
                              of men."

                              LXVI

Then they set up the gallows   on the sandy ground,
High on the field,   the folk of the Jews:
The beam on the hillside;   and God's Bairn was tormented
Thereon, on the cross.   They struck cold iron

Now in their eagerness,   nails sharp and new,
Hard with their hammers,   through His hands and His feet:
Bitter bonds were they.   His blood ran to earth,
The gore of our Good Lord.   But this grim deed He cared
                    not
To avenge 'gainst the Jews,   but He bade God the Father,
The Almighty Lord,   that He be not wrathful
'Gainst these men, this world-folk,   "Since they wit not
                    what they do," quoth He.
Then the war-men dealt out   the weeds of the Lord,
Divided Christ's clothing —   coarse men of the foe —
His fair, rich robes.   But the men could not rightly
Become of one mind   about the division
Until in their crowd   they had cast down lots,
Which of them was to have   this holy garment,
The most winsome of weeds.   The world-folk's herdsman,
The duke himself, hight   that over the head
Of Christ on the cross there be writ   that this be the
                    true king of Jews,
Jesus of Nazareth-burg,   who stood there nailed
On the new gallows   because of grim hatred —
On the beam of the rood.   Then the folk bade him
To change that word, quoth that He Himself   had so said
                    as He wished,
Had spoken so of Himself,   that He wielded power over
                    the people,
Was King over the Jews.   Then Caesar's envoy spoke
                    once again,
The harsh leader of hosts: "Over His head it is now so
                    writ,
So wisely inscribed,   and I choose not to change it."
The people of Jews   then put on each side
Of Christ on the cross   two men condemned for their
                    crimes
And left them there tortured   on the gallows-tree as
                    reward
For their works, for their loathsome deeds.   And the land-
                    folk did speak

Many harsh words of scorn   unto Holy Christ,
And with yelps they did greet Him;   they saw the Best of
                    all Men
Tormented there on the cross: "If Thou beest King over
                    all," quoth they,
"The Son of the Lord,   as Thou Thyself hath spoken,
Save Thou Thyself from Thy suffering.   Make Thyself free of
                    such hate!
Go hence hail and well.   Then will this host,
The bairns of the folk believe Thee."   So also spoke
                    blasphemy
A most arrogant Jew   who stood at the gallows.
"Woe to the world," quoth he,   "if Thou didst wield power
                    over it!
Thou sayest Thou canst   cast down in one day
The high, noble house   of the King of Heaven,
The greatest of stoneworks,   and make it stand once more
On the third day.   Up to this time no man of the people
Hath dared to bring such to pass.   But see, how Thou now
                    standeth in fetters
And in sore distress;   nor canst Thou save e'en Thyself
One whit from this pain."   Then, too, one of the thieves
In fetters there did speak —   when he heard the folk
Uttering wicked words —   for his will was ne'er good,
The thoughts of this thrall.   "If Thou beest King of this
                    folk," quoth he,
"Christ, Son of God,   go Thou down from the cross,
Slip loose from these snares   and save us all,
Help us together.   If Thou beest the Heaven-King,
Wielder over this world,   make it known through Thy works,
Reveal Thyself to these many!"   Then spake the other man
Hanging there who stood   held in his fetters,
Suffering great pain.   "Wherefore wilt thou speak such a
                    word,
Greetest thou Him with such scorn?   Thou standeth here
                    held to the gallows,
Broken on the beam.   We both suffer sorely

Because of our sin: our own deeds themselves
Have brought us our pain.   But He standeth there,
Faultless and free of all sin;   for He Himself
Hath committed no crime;   but for the hate of the crowd
He willingly endureth   dire pain in this world.
I shall most willingly believe," quoth he,   "and shall
                    eagerly bid Him,
The Son of the Lord,   the Warder of Lands,
That Thou thinkest of me   and that Thou beest my help,
O Best of All Rulers,   when Thou reachest Thy realm —
Have mercy on me!"   Then Christ Savior did speak
Unto him with His words.   "Verily I say unto Thee," quoth
                    He,
"That still on this day   thou shalt see God's light
Together with Me   in the kingdom of Heaven,
In Paradise, though thou   art now in such pain."
There stood also Mary,   the mother of Christ,
Bleached pale 'neath the beam,   and beheld her Bairn tortured,
Suffering such agony.   And there were also women there come
With her for love of Him,   who was the Almighty.
And John stood there, too,   the disciple of Christ,
Sadly beneath His Lord;   and his spirit was sore,
Grieved for this death.   Then Christ the Great Lord did
                    speak,
The Mighty One to His mother: "To My disciples
I hereby consign thee,   to him who standeth here before Me.
Enter thou into his household.   Thou shalt have him for a
                    son."
Then He greeted John there,   hight that he care for her
                    well,
Love her so mildly, as one should one's mother,
This maid without stain.   Pure of mind, he received her
Into his care,   as his Lord had commanded.

LXVII

Then at the mid-hour of day   a mighty token
Was wonderously revealed   over the whole of the world,
When they had raised God's Son   onto the gallows,
Christ onto the cross: then it became known everywhere
How the sun was made swarthy,   nor could its fair shimmering,
              light
Shine down any longer,   but its rays were surrounded
With darkness and gloom,   and dim fogs did o'ercast it.
Thus came the dreariest day,   the greatest darkness
Over the whole, wide world,   as long as the All-Wielder
Christ, suffered pain on the cross,   the Richest of Kings,
Till the ninth hour of day.   Then the midsts did divide,
The swarthiness scattered,   and the light of the sun
Appeared clear in the heaven.   Then the Strongest of
              Kings,
The Greatest, cried up to God,   as He stood on the cross,
Fingers and arms fast bound in their fetters.   "Father
              Almighty," cried He,
"Wherefore hast Thou so forsaken Me,   Thou My Dear Lord,
Thou Holy Heaven-King?   And leavest Thy help,
Thy support so far?   I stand 'mid the foe
So terribly tortured."   Then truly the folk of the Jews
Laughed to revile Him.   They heard Holy Christ,
The Lord, before His death,   ask for a drink,
Heard Him say that He thirsted;   but the throng could not
              cease their harrying,
His wicked foes.   But there was in them a great wish
To bring unto Him still   something more of bitterness,
And the sin-minded folk   had mixed for Him
Vinegar, unsweet, and gall,   and a man stood ready —
A right guilty scoundrel   whom they had chosen for this,
Had enticed with their speech,   so that he took a sponge
Loaded with the most loathsome of wines;   on a long shaft
              he put it,
Bound to a beam;   and to God's Bairn he did give it,

Into the mouth of the Mighty One.   Christ saw through this
                              murky deed,
Felt well its treachery —   He no longer cared to taste
Of such bitterness;   but the Bairn of God cried aloud
To His Father in Heaven.   "Into Thy hands I commend Myself,"
                              quoth He,
"My ghost, My spirit unto God's will.   It is now good,
It is ready to come unto Thee."   The Lord of All Peoples
Inclined His head,   and His holy breath
Escaped from His body.   As now the Warder of Lands
Died in His ropes,   there was straightway revealed
A right wonderous token: so that the Wielder's death
Would be made known   to the speechless many
And His end-day fulfilled.   The earth did tremble,
And the high mountains shook,   and the hard stone split
                              open,
The crags on the fields;   and the fair curtain was rent,
Was torn in two down the middle —   that veil in the temple
Which had hung there   unharmed and most wonderously
Broidered for many a day —   for the bairns of mankind,
The people were never   permitted to see what holy things
Hung hidden behind that veil.   Now they could see the
                              hoard:
The Jewish folk could now gaze on it.   And the graves of
                              dead men
Burst open and wide;   and in their bodies
They rose up living   out of the earth —
All through the strength of the Lord —   and were there
                              revealed
As a marvel to men.   This was a mighty thing,
That so much should feel,   should recognize, too,
The death of the Christ: so many a thing that had never
                              spoken
One word to any man in this world.   Verily the folk of the
                              Jews
Saw many strange things;   but their cruel spirits
Had grown so hard in their hearts,   that there was no holy
                              sign,

No token revealed unto them,   which made them trust more
In Christ's might and strength: that He was the King
Over all the peoples of world.   But some spoke with their
                    words,
Some who were set guarding   the bodies there in the ground,
That this was truly   the Son of the All-Wielder,
The Best of All Bairns.   Some beat their breasts sorely —
Some weeping women;   wonderous pain they felt,
Much hurt in their hearts,   at their High Lord's death,
And they were sorely grieved.   Now it was the custom of
                    the Jews,
That they did not leave any prisoner   hanging there longer
On a holy day, except just as long,   until life had glided
                    away,
Till his soul had sunk from him;   and the sly, grim-minded
                    men
In their hatred came closer   to where, along with the
                    Christ,
The two thieves were nailed,   both suffering torture
Along with Him.   They were both still alive,
Until the loathsome   folk of the Jews
Broke their leg-bones,   and both together
Took leave of life,   seeking another light.
But they needed not drive   Lord Christ to His death
With further sins of that sort;   but they found He had
                    fared thence,
His soul had repaired from here   on to the right path,
To long-lasting light.   His limbs had grown cold,
The fire had gone from His flesh;   then one of the folk
                    went up to Him
With hatred of heart;   and in his hand he did bear
A spear, sharp and nailed.   And with sword-strength he did
                    thrust it,
Let the point of the weapon   cut deep in the wound,
So that on one side   Christ's body itself
Was laid open.   The landsmen there saw
That the blood and the water —   both did spring forth,

Did well from the wound,   as was His will,
And as before He had marked it   for the kinship of men,
For the good of the folk-bairns,   and so indeed 'twas
                              fulfilled.

LXVIII

The bright, shining sun   with its beacon of beams
Had sunk down further   close to its seat —
On that gloomy day there did come   a thane of our Lord:
A clever man was he,   a disciple of Christ
For a long time already,   although not many a man
Had ken thereof, since with his words   he had concealed it
                              indeed
From the people of Jews.   Joseph was he hight;
He was his Lord's disciple in secret,   and he wished not to
                              follow this sinful folk
In their works of wickedness;   but amid the Jewish folk
                              he awaited
The holy kingdom of Heaven.   He went hence to speak to the
                              duke,
To make issue with the envoy of Caesar;   and he urged him
                              muchly
To release Christ's body   from the cross, where it stood
                              in torture,
To let the Good Man be lowered   from the gallows and laid
                              in a grave,
Consigned to earth's folds.   And the leader of the folk
Did not wish to deny him his will,   but did grant him the right
To accomplish his deed.   Then he did go forth from there,
Did go to the gallows,   where he knew God's Bairn,
Where he knew the body   of his Lord was hanging.
From the new rood he did take it   and from the nails he
                              freed it,
And into his arms he received it —   as one should do for
                              one's dear lord —
He took the loved body   and wound it with linen

And carried it carefully —   for his Lord was clearly worthy
                                     thereof —
To where they had hewn   a place with their hands,
A spot in the stone,   where still no child of mankind,
No person had ever been buried.   There they placed God's
                                     Bairn,
Committed the holiest of corpses,   as was their custom,
Into the folds of the earth.   And with a rock they did
                                     close
The goodliest of graves.   Grieving, there sat
Women there in their misery,   those who had witnessed all,
The grim death of the Man.   They started to go thence,
The weeping women,   watching most carefully
On what path they should again   go back to the grave.
They had seen sadness   and sorrow aplenty,
Mikil grief of their minds: Mary were they both hight,
These women in misery.   Then was the evening come,
The night with its darkness.   The dire, hating Jews
Gathered again on the morrow,   many together...[1]
Speaking in secret: "What, thou knowest surely,
That through this One man   thy realm was indeed doubt-
                                     rent,
The people confused.   Now lieth He wound-pierced
And buried all deeply.   He ever did say that He would arise
From the dead on the third day.   This many folk do believe.
Many people do mark His words.   Now order thou a watch,
A guard at His grave,   lest His disciples
Steal Him away from the stone,   and say then that He,
Rich and mighty, had risen   from His rest.   Then the
                                     warrior-folk
Will be angered still more,   if they begin to announce that
                                     about."
Then there were people   appointed from the horde of the
                                     Jews,
War-men for the watch.   They went hence with their weapons:

[1] Lucuna in Ms.

They did go to the grave.   There were they to guard
The body of God's Bairn.   So passed by the holy day
Of the Jews and was gone.   They sat over the grave,
The warriors on watch   in the wide, sparkling night,
Biding under their shield-boards,   until the bright day
Came to mankind   over the mid-world here,
Bringing light to the land-folk.   It was not long thereafter
That through God's strength   the spirit returned
Under the hard stone.   The Holy breath
Returned to the body.   The light was revealed
For the boon of mankind,   and many a bolt
Was unlatched on hell's doors,   and the way to Heaven
From the world was fashioned.   Full radiant arose
The Peace-Bairn of God,   and He did go as He willed,
So that the wardens of the grave   could not recognize Him
                even one whit —
That ruthless rabble —   when He rose from the dead,
Arose from His rest.   Outside 'round the grave
The warriors did sit,   the host with their shields,
The folk of the Jews.   The fair sun strode forward,
The clear, winsome light.   And the women went forth,
Going to the grave,   wives of good clan,
The Marys most lovely.   They had sold much treasure
Of silver and gold   to buy salves, had sold
Much of wealth for herbs and for worts.   Whatsoever they
                could gain,
So that they could embalm   the body of their beloved Lord,
The Almighty's Son,   with their herbs and salves,
Him slashed with wounds.   The women sorrowed
So greatly in spirit,   and some of them spoke:
Who would roll it aside, the great stone from the grave
For them, the stone   which they had seen
The men lay over the corpse,   when they had consigned it
Into its nook in the rocks.   When verily now the women
Had gone to the garden,   so that they might see the grave
                itself,
The Almighty's angel did come   from the sky above,

Faring down from the firmament   in a shroud of feathers,
So that the world, the earth   did echo and the men
Became weak in their spirits,   the watchmen of Jews,
And fell down in fright.   They feared they would have
Their lives not much longer.

LXIX

                    The guards lay there,
The thralls, as though dead;   then straightway came uncovered
The great stone from the grave;   for God's angel
Did roll it aside;   and the Lord's radiant herald
Did sit him there on the stone;   in his face, in his deeds —
So that all and each   might see with their eyes —
He was as bright and blithe   as a bolt of lightning.
And his weeds, his vestments   were as the winter-cold snow,
Then they did see him,   sitting there on the stone that was
                    turned —
The women beheld him;   and from the brightness
Great fear struck the wives;   they were sore afraid
And mightily frightened   and dared go no further,
Dared not go to the grave,   until the angel of God,
The Wielder's herald,   did greet them with words,
Quoth that he knew well   what their errand,
Their work and their will,   and the mind of these good
                    wives;
Hight that they fear not,   "For I know ye seek Him,
Your Lord, Savior Christ,   from the city of Nazareth,
Him whom the clans of the Jews   did torture and nail to
                    the cross,
Him sinless they laid in the grave.   He Himself is not
                    there,
But He hath arisen,   and this place standeth empty,
This grave in the grotto.   Now may ye go nearer,
May come much closer;   clearly I know that ye long
To see inside of the stone;   here still is the spot

Where His body was laid."   In their breasts the women,
           wan though they were
And pale, began   to be greatly comforted,
The winsome, fair wives.   A most welcome message
They had heard here —   that which the herald of God,
The All-Wielder's angel, had said.   He hight that they again
Go hence from the grave;   and go to Christ's followers
And say unto His thanes   this word most sooth:
That their Lord Most Beloved,   lo, had arisen from death
Most especially he hight   that unto Simon Peter
Be told with words   this most welcome spell
Of the coming of the Lord: that Christ Himself
Was in Galilee-land,   and there again His retainers,
Disciples shall see Him,   as He Himself did say
With His words of truth.   Just as the wives
Were about to go thence,   there stood there before them
Two angels clad   all in garments of white,
In weeds, shining and winsome,   and with their words
They spoke unto them holy things;   and the hearts of the
           women
Were made anxious with fright,   for they feared to look at
           God's angels,
Could not gaze into the brightness;   for the glory of them
           was too great,
Was too strong to see.   Then the Wielder's heralds spoke
Again unto them   and did ask the women
Why they were come   to seek Christ the Quick
Here 'mid the dead,   the Son of the Master,
Him filled with life.   "Ye shall not find Him
Here in this stony grave.   But He hath arisen
In His body hence;   and this shall ye believe;
And remember these words,   which most verily
He Himself hath oft said,   when He was with you
In Galilee-land: how He would be given over and betrayed,
How He would be sold   to sinful mankind
Into the hand of the hater —   the Most Holy Lord —
So that they would torment Him,   and tack Him to the cross,

Would do Him to death,   and that on the third day
Through the might of Lord God   and for the good of all
                              men,
He would arise, once more living.   That verily hath been
                              done now,
Brought to pass 'mid the people.   Repair ye swiftly —
Haste ye hence, and make this known   to the followers of
                              Him.

LXX

He hath gone on ahead   and is away
In Galilee-land,   and His retainers shall see Him again,
His disciples there."   And straightway this was joy,
Was winsomeness for the women,   when they heard such words
                              spoken,
Making known God's might — yet much frightened were they
                              still,
Filled with a fear of Him;   and they set them forth
To go from the grave;   and unto Christ's disciples they
                              gladly
Did speak of the wonderous sight,   while sorrowing still
They bided such bettering.   To the bastions were come
The Jewish guardsmen, too,   who had sat by the grave
All the long, long night,   had lain in watch o'er the
                              corpse,
O'er the body there buried;   and while they there bided —
They said unto the host of the Jews —   what shock, what
                              fright,
What strange sight came unto them;   and they said also with
                              their words
How it was all so done   with the might of the Lord;
Nor kept they it hidden within their hearts.   And the host
                              of the Jews
Offered to them great treasures   both of silver and of gold,
Bought from them with bright jewels   the promise that they
                              would not tell,

Nor make this known to the many;   "But say ye that
            with weary minds
Ye did fall asleep;   and there did come His disciples
And stole Him away from behind the stone.   Do ye this
            ever with zeal,
Go on in eagerness;   and if the folk-leader doth gain
            knowledge thereof,
We shall help you against that high lord,   so that no whit
            of harm,
No grief shall o'ertake you."   Then they took great treasures,
Precious jewels from the people,   but pursued the course
            they had begun,
For they had no power o'er their will;   but they broadcast
            it widely
To the folk in the land,   that such lies were here spread
About the Holy Lord.   Then were the hearts once more
            healed
For the disciples of Christ,   when they did hear the good
            wives
Give praise unto God's power.   Then their hearts grew
            joyous,
And both of them ran,   rushing swiftly up to the grave,
Until soon after   Simon Peter did come,
Earl famed for his strength;   and he went on
Going straight to the grave;   and he saw there the garments
Of God's Bairn, of His Lord,   the linen lying there,
The beautiful shroud   with which His body
Had been bound so fairly.   Far from that lay the cloth
With which Holy Christ's head   had been covered,
Our Mighty Lord's face,   when He lay in this rest.
Then John also did go   inside the grave
To see this strange thing;   and straightway thereafter
His belief was unlocked, so that he knew   that He would
            again come to this light —
His Lord most dear,   would arise from the dead
Up out of this earth.   Then they again went away,
The twain, Peter and John,   and the retainers, disciples

Of Christ came together.   With care-filled heart
One of the women stood   for a second time
Groaning over the grave — her spirit was grieved —
It was Mary Magdelan —   the thoughts of her mind,
Of her soul were seized with sorrow,   nor knew she where she
                    should seek Him,
The Lord who would grant her help.   She could not leave
                off her lamenting;
The woman could not cease her weeping.   Nor knew she where
                she could turn.
The thoughts of her mind were distracted.   Then she saw
                Mighty Christ
Standing there —   although she could not perceive Him
As someone she knew,   until He so wished to reveal it,
Until He would say who He was.   He asked what she was be-
                moaning so sorely.
So terribly there with her hot tears.   She told Him she verily
                knew not
Where they had taken her Lord.   "If Thou can'st show me,
O my Lord, if I may ask Thee,   if Thou hast taken Him
                away
From behind these rocks,   then instruct me with words —
                that would be my greatest wish:
That I could see Him myself."   She knew not 'twas the
                Son of the Lord
Whom she was greeting with her good speech.   She weened
                'twas a gardener,
Yard-guardian of his master.   Then the Holy Lord did
                greet her
By name, the Best of All Saviors.   And straightway she
                came closer,
The wife, with good will,   and recognized her Savior
                Himself.
In her love she could not refrain,   but with her hands
                she longed to hold Him,
The woman to touch the World-Lord.   "Not yet," quoth He,
                "have I risen to Him, the
                Heavenly Father.

But haste thou now swiftly,   and make it known to the earls,
To My brethren here,   that I will see Him,
The All-Wielder,   Father of us both,
Yours and Mine, too,   Mighty God, true and fast."

LXXI

The woman was in raptures   that she could proclaim such
                              joy,
Could say of Him, that He was sound   and was well. Straight-
                    way the woman
Was eager to announce this message,   and to the earls she
                         did bring it,
Welcome tidings to the warriors: that All-Wielding
                    Christ
She had seen well and sound;   and she said that He Himself
Had granted unto her this glorious day.   They still wished
                    not to trust
The woman's word, that she brought   such a message so
                         welcome
Verily from the Son of God,   and they sat grieved of
                    heart,
The heroes lamenting.   Then Holy Christ,
The Lord, revealed Himself   openly another time
Since He rose from the dead.   He did so do this
For the sake of the woman,   that He met them on the way.
He spoke to them as One whom they knew,   and they bent
                    their knee before Him,
Fell at His feet.   He hight that no fear
Should they bear in their breast.   "But unto My brethren
Shall ye make known My message,   that they shall follow
Into Galilee-land.   There shall I meet them again."
On that selfsame day   of the disciples
Two earls early   already that morn
Were faring on business.   They wished to find them the
                         fortress
Of Emaus, the castle.   Among the men many

204

A word did begin to wax,   as they fared on their way,
God's Holy Son. Still could they   not know Him one whit,
Him the Mighty and Strong.   He had no wish to reveal Him-
self unto them.
Still He went along with them,   and He asked about what
they were speaking:
"Why go ye so groaning," quoth He,   "Ye twain with such
grieving hearts
And souls filled with sorrow?"   They straightway replied
unto Him,
The earls then gave answer: "Why dost Thou ask so?"
quoth they.
"Art Thou from Jerusalem   from the folk of the Jews?"...[1]
The Holy Ghost   from the fields of Heaven
With the great strength of Lord God."   Now He took those
good earls,
His disciples there   and He did lead them out,
Until He brought them   to Bethany.
There He held up His hands   and made them holy:
With His words He did bless them.   Then He went Him hence,
Sought the high realm of Heaven   and His holy throne.
And there He doth sit   on the right side of God,
The Father Almighty.   And from there All-Wielding Christ
Gazes down and sees   what power doth surround the world.
Then on the same spot   the disciples good
Fell down in prayer,   and the followers of Christ
Fared rejoicing again   to Jerusalem.
To the city they hastened,   and their hearts were joyous.
In the temple they tarried.   Truly the strength of the
Wielder...

[1] Lacuna in Ms.

UNIVERSITY OF NORTH CAROLINA
STUDIES IN THE GERMANIC LANGUAGES
AND LITERATURES